interchange
FIFTH EDITION

2B

Student's Book

Jack C. Richards
with Jonathan Hull and Susan Proctor

WITH ONLINE SELF-STUDY
AND ONLINE WORKBOOK

CAMBRIDGE
UNIVERSITY PRESS

University Printing House, Cambridge CB2 8BS, United Kingdom

One Liberty Plaza, 20th Floor, New York, NY 10006, USA

477 Williamstown Road, Port Melbourne, VIC 3207, Australia

314–321, 3rd Floor, Plot 3, Splendor Forum, Jasola District Centre, New Delhi – 110025, India

79 Anson Road, #06–04/06, Singapore 079906

Cambridge University Press is part of the University of Cambridge.

It furthers the University's mission by disseminating knowledge in the pursuit of education, learning and research at the highest international levels of excellence.

www.cambridge.org
Information on this title: www.cambridge.org/9781316620373

© Cambridge University Press 2013, 2017

This publication is in copyright. Subject to statutory exception and to the provisions of relevant collective licensing agreements, no reproduction of any part may take place without the written permission of Cambridge University Press.

First published 2013

20 19 18 17 16 15 14 13 12 11 10 9 8 7 6 5 4

Printed in the United Kingdom by Latimer Trend

A catalogue record for this publication is available from the British Library

ISBN	9781316620236	Student's Book 2 with Online Self-Study
ISBN	9781316620250	Student's Book 2A with Online Self-Study
ISBN	9781316620328	Student's Book 2B with Online Self-Study
ISBN	9781316620342	Student's Book 2 with Online Self-Study and Online Workbook
ISBN	9781316620366	Student's Book 2A with Online Self-Study and Online Workbook
ISBN	9781316620373	Student's Book 2B with Online Self-Study and Online Workbook
ISBN	9781316622698	Workbook 2
ISBN	9781316622704	Workbook 2A
ISBN	9781316622711	Workbook 2B
ISBN	9781316622728	Teacher's Edition 2 with Complete Assessment Program
ISBN	9781316622285	Class Audio 2 CDs
ISBN	9781316623992	Full Contact 2 with Online Self-Study
ISBN	9781316624005	Full Contact 2A with Online Self-Study
ISBN	9781316624029	Full Contact 2B with Online Self-Study
ISBN	9781108403061	Presentation Plus 2

Additional resources for this publication at www.cambridge.org/interchange

Cambridge University Press has no responsibility for the persistence or accuracy of URLs for external or third-party internet websites referred to in this publication, and does not guarantee that any content on such websites is, or will remain, accurate or appropriate. Information regarding prices, travel timetables, and other factual information given in this work is correct at the time of first printing but Cambridge University Press does not guarantee the accuracy of such information thereafter.

Informed by teachers

Teachers from all over the world helped develop *Interchange Fifth Edition*. They looked at everything – from the color of the designs to the topics in the conversations – in order to make sure that this course will work in the classroom. We heard from 1,500 teachers in:

- Surveys
- Focus Groups
- In-Depth Reviews

We appreciate the help and input from everyone. In particular, we'd like to give the following people our special thanks:

Jader Franceschi, **Actúa Idiomas,** Bento Gonçalves, Rio Grande do Sul, Brazil

Juliana Dos Santos Voltan Costa, **Actus Idiomas,** São Paulo, Brazil

Ella Osorio, **Angelo State University,** San Angelo, TX, US

Mary Hunter, **Angelo State University,** San Angelo, TX, US

Mario César González, **Angloamericano de Monterrey, SC,** Monterrey, Mexico

Samantha Shipman, **Auburn High School,** Auburn, AL, US

Linda, **Bernick Language School,** Radford, VA, US

Dave Lowrance, **Bethesda University of California,** Yorba Linda, CA, US

Tajbakhsh Hosseini, **Bezmialem Vakif University,** Istanbul, Turkey

Dilek Gercek, **Bil English,** Izmir, Turkey

Erkan Kolat, **Biruni University, ELT,** Istanbul, Turkey

Nika Gutkowska, **Bluedata International,** New York, NY, US

Daniel Alcocer Gómez, **Cecati 92,** Guadalupe, Nuevo León, Mexico

Samantha Webb, **Central Middle School,** Milton-Freewater, OR, US

Verónica Salgado, **Centro Anglo Americano,** Cuernavaca, Mexico

Ana Rivadeneira Martínez and Georgia P. de Machuca, **Centro de Educación Continua – Universidad Politécnica del Ecuador,** Quito, Ecuador

Anderson Francisco Guimerães Maia, **Centro Cultural Brasil Estados Unidos,** Belém, Brazil

Rosana Mariano, **Centro Paula Souza,** São Paulo, Brazil

Carlos de la Paz Arroyo, Teresa Noemí Parra Alarcón, Gilberto Bastida Gaytan, Manuel Esquivel Román, and Rosa Cepeda Tapia, **Centro Universitario Angloamericano,** Cuernavaca, Morelos, Mexico

Antonio Almeida, **CETEC,** Morelos, Mexico

Cinthia Ferreira, **Cinthia Ferreira Languages Services,** Toronto, ON, Canada

Phil Thomas and Sérgio Sanchez, **CLS Canadian Language School,** São Paulo, Brazil

Celia Concannon, **Cochise College,** Nogales, AZ, US

Maria do Carmo Rocha and CAOP English team, **Colégio Arquidiocesano Ouro Preto – Unidade Cônego Paulo Dilascio,** Ouro Preto, Brazil

Kim Rodriguez, **College of Charleston North,** Charleston, SC, US

Jesús Leza Alvarado, **Coparmex English Institute,** Monterrey, Mexico

John Partain, **Cortazar,** Guanajuato, Mexico

Alexander Palencia Navas, **Cursos de Lenguas, Universidad del Atlántico,** Barranquilla, Colombia

Kenneth Johan Gerardo Steenhuisen Cera, Melfi Osvaldo Guzman Triana, and Carlos Alberto Algarín Jiminez, **Cursos de Lenguas Extranjeras Universidad del Atlantico,** Barranquilla, Colombia

Jane P Kerford, **East Los Angeles College,** Pasadena, CA, US

Daniela, **East Village,** Campinas, São Paulo, Brazil

Rosalva Camacho Orduño, **Easy English for Groups S.A. de C.V.,** Monterrey, Nuevo León, Mexico

Adonis Gimenez Fusetti, **Easy Way Idiomas,** Ibiúna, Brazil

Eileen Thompson, **Edison Community College,** Piqua, OH, US

Ahminne Handeri O.L Froede, **Englishouse escola de idiomas,** Teófilo Otoni, Brazil

Ana Luz Delgado-Izazola, **Escuela Nacional Preparatoria 5, UNAM,** Mexico City, Mexico

Nancy Alarcón Mendoza, **Facultad de Estudios Superiores Zaragoza, UNAM,** Mexico City, Mexico

Marcilio N. Barros, **Fast English USA,** Campinas, São Paulo, Brazil

Greta Douthat, **FCI Ashland,** Ashland, KY, US

Carlos Lizárraga González, **Grupo Educativo Anglo Americano, S.C.,** Mexico City, Mexico

Hugo Fernando Alcántar Valle, **Instituto Politécnico Nacional, Escuela Superior de Comercio y Administración-Unidad Santotomás, Celex Esca Santo Tomás,** Mexico City, Mexico

Sueli Nascimento, **Instituto Superior de Educação do Rio de Janeiro,** Rio de Janeiro, Brazil

Elsa F Monteverde, **International Academic Services,** Miami, FL, US

Laura Anand, **Irvine Adult School,** Irvine, CA, US

Prof. Marli T. Fernandes (principal) and Prof. Dr. Jefferson J. Fernandes (pedagogue), **Jefferson Idiomas,** São Paulo, Brazil

Herman Bartelen, **Kanda Gaigo Gakuin,** Tokyo, Japan

Cassia Silva, **Key Languages,** Key Biscayne, FL, US

Sister Mary Hope, **Kyoto Notre Dame Joshi Gakuin,** Kyoto, Japan

Nate Freedman, **LAL Language Centres,** Boston, MA, US

Richard Janzen, **Langley Secondary School,** Abbotsford, BC, Canada

Christina Abel Gabardo, **Language House,** Campo Largo, Brazil

Ivonne Castro, **Learn English International,** Cali, Colombia

Julio Cesar Maciel Rodrigues, **Liberty Centro de Línguas,** São Paulo, Brazil

Ann Gibson, **Maynard High School,** Maynard, MA, US

Martin Darling, **Meiji Gakuin Daigaku,** Tokyo, Japan

Dax Thomas, **Meiji Gakuin Daigaku,** Yokohama, Kanagawa, Japan

Derya Budak, **Mevlana University,** Konya, Turkey

B Sullivan, **Miami Valley Career Technical Center International Program,** Dayton, OH, US

Julio Velazquez, **Milo Language Center,** Weston, FL, US

Daiane Siqueira da Silva, Luiz Carlos Buontempo, Marlete Avelina de Oliveira Cunha, Marcos Paulo Segatti, Morgana Eveline de Oliveira, Nadia Lia Gino Alo, and Paul Hyde Budgen, **New Interchange-Escola de Idiomas,** São Paulo, Brazil

Patrícia França Furtado da Costa, Juiz de Fora, Brazil Patricia Servín

Chris Pollard, **North West Regional College SK,** North Battleford, SK, Canada

Olga Amy, **Notre Dame High School,** Red Deer, Canada

Amy Garrett, **Ouachita Baptist University,** Arkadelphia, AR, US

Mervin Curry, **Palm Beach State College,** Boca Raton, FL, US

Julie Barros, **Quality English Studio,** Guarulhos, São Paulo, Brazil

Teodoro González Saldaña and Jesús Monserrrta Mata Franco, **Race Idiomas,** Mexico City, Mexico

Autumn Westphal and Noga La`or, **Rennert International,** New York, NY, US

Antonio Gallo and Javy Palau, **Rigby Idiomas,** Monterrey, Mexico Tatiane Gabriela Sperb do Nascimento, **Right Way,** Igrejinha, Brazil

Mustafa Akgül, **Selahaddin Eyyubi Universitesi,** Diyarbakır, Turkey

James Drury M. Fonseca, **Senac Idiomas Fortaleza,** Fortaleza, Ceara, Brazil

Manoel Fialho S Neto, **Senac – PE,** Recife, Brazil

Jane Imber, **Small World,** Lawrence, KS, US

Tony Torres, **South Texas College,** McAllen, TX, US

Janet Rose, **Tennessee Foreign Language Institute,** College Grove, TN, US

Todd Enslen, **Tohoku University,** Sendai, Miyagi, Japan

Daniel Murray, **Torrance Adult School,** Torrance, CA, US

Juan Manuel Pulido Mendoza, **Universidad del Atlántico,** Barranquilla, Colombia

Juan Carlos Vargas Millán, **Universidad Libre Seccional Cali,** Cali (Valle del Cauca), Colombia

Carmen Cecilia Llanos Ospina, **Universidad Libre Seccional Cali,** Cali, Colombia

Jorge Noriega Zenteno, **Universidad Politécnica del Valle de México,** Estado de México, Mexico

Aimee Natasha Holguin S., **Universidad Politécnica del Valle de México UPVM,** Tultitlàn Estado de México, Mexico

Christian Selene Bernal Barraza, **UPVM Universidad Politécnica del Valle de México,** Ecatepec, Mexico

Lizeth Ramos Acosta, **Universidad Santiago de Cali,** Cali, Colombia

Silvana Dushku, **University of Illinois Champaign,** IL, US

Deirdre McMurtry, **University of Nebraska – Omaha,** Omaha, NE, US

Jason E Mower, **University of Utah,** Salt Lake City, UT, US

Paul Chugg, **Vanguard Taylor Language Institute,** Edmonton, Alberta, Canada

Henry Mulak, **Varsity Tutors,** Los Angeles, CA, US

Shirlei Strucker Calgaro and Hugo Guilherme Karrer, **VIP Centro de Idiomas,** Panambi, Rio Grande do Sul, Brazil

Eleanor Kelly, **Waseda Daigaku Extension Centre,** Tokyo, Japan

Sherry Ashworth, **Wichita State University,** Wichita, KS, US

Laine Bourdene, **William Carey University,** Hattiesburg, MS, US

Serap Aydın, Istanbul, Turkey

Liliana Covino, Guarulhos, Brazil

Yannuarys Jiménez, Barranquilla, Colombia

Juliana Morais Pazzini, Toronto, ON, Canada

Marlon Sanches, Montreal, Canada

Additional content contributed by Kenna Bourke, Inara Couto, Nic Harris, Greg Manin, Ashleigh Martinez, Laura McKenzie, Paul McIntyre, Clara Prado, Lynne Robertson, Mari Vargo, Theo Walker, and Maria Lucia Zaorob.

Classroom Language Student questions

Plan of Book 2B

Titles/Topics	Speaking	Grammar
UNIT 9 — PAGES 58–63 **Only time will tell.** Life in the past, present, and future; changes and contrasts; consequences	Talking about change; comparing time periods; describing possible consequences	Time contrasts; conditional sentences with *if* clauses
UNIT 10 — PAGES 64–69 **I like working with people.** Abilities and skills; job preferences; personality traits; careers	Describing abilities and skills; talking about job preferences; describing personality traits	Gerunds; short responses; clauses with *because*
PROGRESS CHECK — PAGES 70–71		
UNIT 11 — PAGES 72–77 **It's really worth seeing!** Landmarks and monuments; world knowledge	Talking about landmarks and monuments; describing countries; discussing facts	Passive with *by* (simple past); passive without *by* (simple present)
UNIT 12 — PAGES 78–83 **It's a long story.** Storytelling; unexpected recent past events	Describing recent past events and experiences; discussing someone's activities lately	Past continuous vs. simple past; present perfect continuous
PROGRESS CHECK — PAGES 84–85		
UNIT 13 — PAGES 86–91 **That's entertainment!** Entertainment; movies and books; reactions and opinions	Describing movies and books; talking about actors and actresses; asking for and giving reactions and opinions	Participles as adjectives; relative pronouns for people and things
UNIT 14 — PAGES 92–97 **Now I get it!** Nonverbal communication; gestures and meaning; signs; drawing conclusions	Interpreting body language; explaining gestures and meanings; describing acceptable and prohibited behavior in different situations; asking about signs and their meaning	Modals and adverbs: *might, may, could, must, maybe, perhaps, probably, definitely*; permission, obligation, and prohibition
PROGRESS CHECK — PAGES 98–99		
UNIT 15 — PAGES 100–105 **I wouldn't have done that.** Money; hopes; predicaments; speculations	Speculating about past and future events; describing a predicament; giving advice and suggestions	Unreal conditional sentences with *if* clauses; past modals
UNIT 16 — PAGES 106–111 **Making excuses** Requests; excuses; invitations	Reporting what people said; making polite requests; making invitations and excuses	Reported speech: requests and statements
PROGRESS CHECK — PAGES 112–113		
GRAMMAR PLUS — PAGES 140–151		

Pronunciation/Listening	Writing/Reading	Interchange Activity
Intonation in statements with time phrases Listening to people talk about changes	Writing a paragraph describing a person's past, present, and possible future "Aquaviva: Fighting for a Future": Reading about a town's attempt to attract new residents	"Cause and effect": Agreeing and disagreeing with classmates **PAGE 123**
Unreleased and released /t/ and /d/ Listening to people talk about their job preferences	Writing a an online cover letter for a job application "Global Work Solutions": Reading about understanding cultural differences in an international company	"You're hired.": Interviewing for a job **PAGE 124**
The letter o Listening to descriptions of monuments; listening for information about a country	Writing an introduction to an online city guide Reading about unusual museums	"True or false?": Sharing information about famous works **PAGE 125**
Contrastive stress in responses Listening to stories about unexpected experiences	Writing a description of a recent experience "Breaking Down the Sound of Silence": Reading about an unusual rock band	"It's my life.": Playing a board game to share past experiences **PAGE 126**
Emphatic stress Listening for opinions; listening to a movie review	Writing a movie review "The Real Art of Acting": Reading about unpleasant experiences actors put themselves through	"It was hilarious!": Asking classmates' opinions about movies, TV shows, and celebrities **PAGE 127**
Pitch Listening to people talk about the meaning of signs	Writing a list of rules "Understanding Idioms": Reading about idioms and their meaning	"Casual observers": Interpreting body language **PAGE 128**
Reduction of *have* Listening to people talk about predicaments; listening to a call-in radio show	Writing a blog post asking for advice "TOPTIPS.COM": Reading an online advice forum	"Tough choices": Deciding what to do in a difficult situation **PAGE 130**
Reduction of *had* and *would* Listening for excuses	Writing a report about people's responses to a survey "A Good Excuse for a Day Off Work": Reading about taking a sick day	"Just a bunch of excuses": Discussing calendar conflicts and making up excuses **PAGES 129, 131**

Plan of Book 2B

9 Only time will tell.

▶ Discuss life in different times
▶ Discuss consequences

1 SNAPSHOT

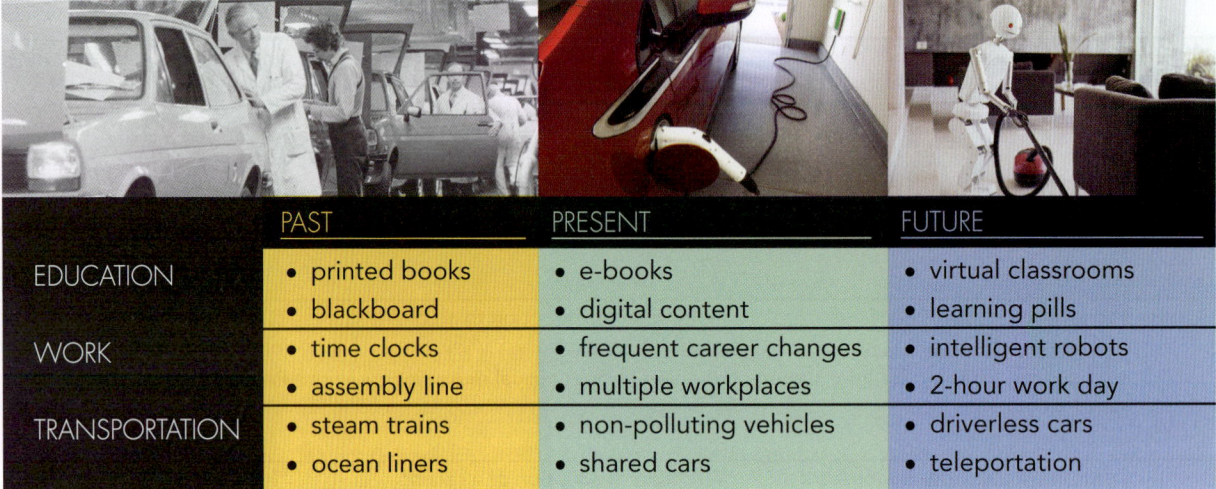

	PAST	PRESENT	FUTURE
EDUCATION	• printed books • blackboard	• e-books • digital content	• virtual classrooms • learning pills
WORK	• time clocks • assembly line	• frequent career changes • multiple workplaces	• intelligent robots • 2-hour work day
TRANSPORTATION	• steam trains • ocean liners	• non-polluting vehicles • shared cars	• driverless cars • teleportation

Which of these changes are the most important? How have they affected the way we live?
Do you think any of the future developments could happen in your lifetime?
Can you think of two other developments that could happen in the future?

2 CONVERSATION That's a thing of the past!

A Listen and practice.

Tom: I hardly recognize our old neighborhood. A few years ago, there were just houses around here.
Mia: I know. They're building a lot of new apartments. The whole neighborhood's different.
Tom: Remember the little burger restaurant we used to go to after school, Hamburger Heaven?
Mia: Of course . . . Now it's another office tower. And I hear they're tearing down our high school. They're going to build a shopping mall.
Tom: That's such a shame. Pretty soon the neighborhood will just be a bunch of malls. And maybe there won't be any schools anymore.
Mia: Probably not. Kids will study from their computers anywhere they want.
Tom: So they won't hang out with their friends after school? That's too bad. I enjoyed meeting our friends at that burger place after class.
Mia: Seriously? That's a thing of the past! Nowadays, kids only meet online.

B Listen to the rest of the conversation. What else has changed in their neighborhood?

3 GRAMMAR FOCUS

Time contrasts

Past	Present	Future
A few years ago, there **were** just houses here.	These days, they**'re building** lots of apartments.	Soon, there **will be** apartment blocks everywhere.
We **used to go** to a burger place after class every day.	Today, people **order** food from their phones.	In the future, restaurants **might not exist**.
In the past, kids **used to hang out** with friends after school.	Nowadays, kids only **meet** online.	In a few years, we **are going to have** virtual friends.

GRAMMAR PLUS see page 140

A Complete the sentences in column A with the appropriate information from column B. Then compare with a partner.

A
1. In the early 1990s, ___
2. Before the airplane, ___
3. Before there were supermarkets, ___
4. In many companies these days, ___
5. In most big cities nowadays, ___
6. In many schools today, ___
7. In the next 100 years, ___
8. Sometime in the near future, ___

B
a. students have their own tablets.
b. pollution is becoming a serious problem.
c. there will probably be cities in space.
d. few people had cell phones.
e. people used to shop at small grocery stores.
f. women still receive lower salaries than men.
g. doctors might find a cure for the common cold.
h. ocean liners were the only way to travel across the Atlantic.

B Complete four of the phrases in part A, column A, with your own ideas. Then compare with a partner.

4 PRONUNCIATION Intonation in statements with time phrases

A Listen and practice. Notice the intonation in these statements beginning with a time phrase.

In the past, few women went to college.

Today, there are more women than men in college in the United States.

In the future, women all over the world will go to college.

B **PAIR WORK** Complete these statements with your own information. Then read your statements to a partner. Pay attention to intonation.

As a child, I used to . . .   These days, . . .
Five years ago, I . . .   In five years, I'll . . .
Nowadays, I . . .   In ten years, I might . . .

Only time will tell

5 LISTENING On the other side of the world

A Listen to Katie talk to her grandfather about an upcoming trip. Check (✓) the three concerns her grandfather has about the trip.

Concern
1. ☐ language   ☐ transportation
2. ☐ meeting people   ☐ money
3. ☐ communication ☐ food

Katie's response
_____
_____
_____

B Listen again. Write what Katie says in response to these concerns.

C PAIR WORK What other problems might someone experience when they travel to another country? How might these problems change in the future?

6 SPEAKING Not anymore.

GROUP WORK How have things changed? How will things be different in the future? Choose four of these topics. Then discuss the questions below.

communications   education   housing
entertainment   fashion   shopping
environment   food   traveling
health

What was it like in the past?
What is it like today?
What will it be like in the future?

A: In the past, people cooked all their meals at home.
B: Not anymore. Nowadays, we eat takeout food all the time.
C: In the future, . . .

7 WRITING He's changed a lot.

A PAIR WORK Interview your partner about his or her past, present, and hopes for the future.

B Write a paragraph describing how your partner has changed. Make some predictions about the future. Don't write your partner's name.

> This person came to our school about two years ago. He used to be a little shy in class, and he didn't have many friends. Now, he's on the basketball team and he is very popular. He's a very talented player and, someday, he'll play on the national team. He'll be famous and very rich. I think he'll . . .

C CLASS ACTIVITY Read your paragraph to the class. Can they guess who it is about?

8 PERSPECTIVES Making the big bucks

A Listen to some possible consequences of getting a high-paying job. Check (✓) the statements you agree with.

If you get a high-paying job, . . .

- ☐ your friends might ask you for a loan.
- ☐ you'll have a lot of money to spend.
- ☐ more people may want to be your friend.
- ☐ you won't have much time for your family.
- ☐ you'll be able to buy anything you want.
- ☐ you won't be able to take long vacations.
- ☐ you'll have to pay higher taxes.
- ☐ you won't have to worry about the future.

B PAIR WORK Look at the statements again. Which are advantages of getting a high-paying job? Which are disadvantages?

"The first one is a disadvantage. I'd like to help my friends, but I wouldn't like to lend them money."

9 GRAMMAR FOCUS

Conditional sentences with *if* clauses

Possible situation (present)	Consequence (future with *will*, *may*, or *might*)
If you **get** a high-paying job,	you**'ll have** more cash to spend.
If you **have** more cash to spend,	you**'ll be able to buy** anything you want.
If you **can buy** anything you want,	you **won't save** your money.
If you **don't save** your money,	you **may have to get** a weekend job.
If you **have to get** a weekend job,	you **might not have** any free time.

GRAMMAR PLUS see page 140

A Match the *if* clauses in column A with the appropriate consequences from column B. Then compare with a partner.

A
1. If you eat less fast food, ___
2. If you walk to work every day, ___
3. If you don't get enough sleep, ___
4. If you change jobs, ___
5. If you don't study regularly, ___
6. If you travel abroad, ___

B
a. you may not learn to speak fluently.
b. you might feel a lot healthier.
c. you'll stay in shape without joining a gym.
d. you'll be able to experience a new culture.
e. you won't be able to stay awake in class.
f. you may not like it better than your old one.

B Add your own consequences to the *if* clauses in column A. Then practice with a partner.

"If you eat less fast food, you will probably live longer."

Only time will tell.

10 WORD POWER Collocations

A PAIR WORK Find phrases from the list that usually go with each verb.
(Sometimes more than one answer is possible.)

a club	a gym	in shape	money	tired
✓ a degree	a living	into college	stressed	work experience
a group	energy	jealous	time	your own money

earn   *a degree*   _____   _____
get   _____   _____   _____
join   _____   _____   _____
spend   _____   _____   _____
feel   _____   _____   _____

B GROUP WORK Share your answers with the group. Can you add one more phrase to each verb?

11 SPEAKING Who knows what will happen?

A GROUP WORK Choose three possible events from below. One student completes an event with a consequence. The next student adds a consequence. Suggest at least five consequences.

fall in love   get a part-time job
join a gym   move to a foreign country
study very hard

If you fall in love, you'll probably want to get married.

If you get married, you'll have to earn your own money.

If you want to earn your own money, you'll need to get a job.

If you get a job, you may spend less time at the gym.

If you spend less time at the gym, you won't keep in shape.

B CLASS ACTIVITY Who has the most interesting consequences for each event?

12 INTERCHANGE 9 Cause and effect

Give your opinion about some issues. Go to Interchange 9 on page 123.

13 READING

A Scan the article. Where is Aguaviva? Who is Luis Bricio?

AGUAVIVA: FIGHTING FOR A FUTURE

Twenty years ago, Aguaviva, a small village in the north of Spain, was dying. Young people wanted more opportunities, so they moved away to the cities. By 1991, there were only 618 people left, and most of them were old. Many of the houses were empty and falling down, and the local school had very few children. Aguaviva's future looked dark.

In 2000, the mayor, Luis Bricio, decided something had to change. He wondered, "How can I bring this place back to life?" He knew the village needed people, but from where? Then he had a brilliant idea. He flew 6,300 miles to Buenos Aires and started telling everyone about Aguaviva. He spoke on the radio and put advertisements in newspapers. The ads said, "If you are married with two children under the age of 12, we'll offer you a home, a job, free health care and education for at least five years." The following year, he did the same thing in Romania.

Many families accepted the offer and Aguaviva began to change. The village school went from having 37 students to more than 80 in three years. The sound of children shouting and playing has made the local people feel so much younger. The economy began to improve, too. There was work for builders repairing the old houses, and a factory making electrical parts for cars opened.

Of course, not everything was easy. The people from Buenos Aires were used to a big city, so living in a small village with little public transportation was difficult at first. The Romanians had to learn a new language. And they all missed their family and friends back home. But everybody had new opportunities, too. Before, many of the parents had worried about finding a job and having enough money to look after their children. After moving to Spain, their future looked brighter. Many of them thought, "We're going to stay here for many years – this place will be our home."

B Read the article. Then answer the questions.

1. Why did young people start leaving Aguaviva?
2. How did Luis Bricio try to attract people to Aguaviva?
3. How did the school change after the year 2000?
4. What kinds of new jobs were there in Aguaviva?
5. What problems did the families from Argentina and Romania have?

C Who would make the following comments? Choose the correct words from the box.

| Luis Bricio | young people from Aguaviva |
| elderly people from Aguaviva | new immigrants |

1. "I'm not going back home because life is better here."
2. "I can't stay here. There are no jobs for people of my age."
3. "I'm going to make this village a better place."
4. "I love having all these kids around me – I don't feel so old."

D Do you think Luis Bricio had a good idea? Would you move to a place like this? What would you miss most about home?

Only time will tell.

10 I like working with people.

▸ Discuss job skills
▸ Discuss kinds of jobs

1 SNAPSHOT

21ST CENTURY SKILLS

- [ ] Can you use technology to find the information you need?
- [ ] Can you evaluate the information you find?
- [ ] Do you work well with different kinds of people?
- [ ] Can you communicate with people from different cultures?
- [ ] Are you good at analyzing and solving problems?
- [ ] Can you develop new ideas?
- [ ] Do you enjoy learning new things?
- [ ] Can you teach others how to do things?

Which of these skills do you think are most important for work? in life? Why?
Check (✓) the skills that you think you have.
Look at the skills you checked. What jobs do you think you might be good at?

2 CONVERSATION I love playing video games.

▶ **A** Listen and practice.

Mai: What are you doing this summer?
Jeff: Nothing much. I'm broke. I need to find a job!
Mai: So do I. Have you seen anything interesting?
Jeff: No, not yet.
Mai: Why don't you get a job at your uncle's restaurant?
Jeff: No way. They're open evenings and weekends, and I hate working on weekends.
Mai: Well, I don't mind working on weekends. Besides, I really enjoy working with people. Do you think he would give me a job?
Jeff: Why don't you go over this weekend and talk to him?
Mai: Yeah. I'll do that. Oh, I found one for you: video game tester.
Jeff: That sounds like fun. I love playing video games. I'll check that one out.

▶ **B** Listen to the rest of the conversation. What is one problem with the job? What does Jeff decide to do?

3 GRAMMAR FOCUS

Gerunds; short responses

Affirmative statements with gerunds	Agree	Disagree	Other verbs or phrases followed by gerunds
I love playing video games.	So do I.	I don't.	like
I hate working on weekends.	So do I.	Really? I like it.	enjoy
I'm good at solving problems.	So am I.	Oh, I'm not.	be interested in
Negative statements with gerunds			
I don't mind working evenings.	Neither do I.	I do.	
I'm not good at selling.	Neither am I.	Well, I am.	
I can't stand commuting.	Neither can I.	Oh, I don't mind it.	

GRAMMAR PLUS see page 141

A PAIR WORK Match the phrases in columns A and B to make statements about yourself. Then take turns reading your sentences and giving short responses.

A
1. I can't stand ____
2. I'm not very good at ____
3. I'm good at ____
4. I don't like ____
5. I hate ____
6. I'm interested in ____
7. I don't mind ____
8. I enjoy ____

B
a. working the night shift.
b. solving other people's problems.
c. working alone.
d. sitting in long meetings.
e. working on weekends.
f. speaking in public.
g. managing my time.
h. learning foreign languages.

A: I can't stand sitting in long meetings.
B: Neither can I.

B GROUP WORK Complete the phrases in column A with your own information. Then take turns reading your statements. Ask questions to get more information.

4 PRONUNCIATION Unreleased and released /t/ and /d/

A Listen and practice. Notice that when the sound /t/ or /d/ at the end of a word is followed by a consonant, it's unreleased. When it is followed by a vowel sound, it's released.

Unreleased
She's not good at dealing with stress.
I hate working on Sundays.
You need to manage money well.

Released
He's not a good artist.
They really hate it!
I need a cup of coffee.

B PAIR WORK Write three sentences starting with *I'm not very good at* and *I don't mind*. Then practice the sentences. Pay attention to the unreleased and released sounds /t/ and /d/.

I like working with people. **65**

5 SPEAKING Do what you love.

A PAIR WORK How does your partner feel about doing these things? Interview your partner. Check (✓) his or her answers.

How do you feel about . . . ?	I enjoy it.	I don't mind it.	I hate it.
dealing with the public	☐	☐	☐
working alone	☐	☐	☐
being part of a team	☐	☐	☐
meeting deadlines	☐	☐	☐
leading a team	☐	☐	☐
working on weekends	☐	☐	☐
learning new skills	☐	☐	☐
doing the same thing every day	☐	☐	☐
traveling	☐	☐	☐
making decisions	☐	☐	☐
helping people	☐	☐	☐
solving problems	☐	☐	☐

B PAIR WORK Look back at the information in part A. Suggest a job for your partner.

A: You enjoy dealing with the public, and you hate working alone. You'd be a good salesperson.
B: But I hate working on weekends.
A: Maybe you could . . .

6 LISTENING My ideal career

A Listen to people talk about the kind of work they are looking for. Then check (✓) each person's ideal job.

1. Alex
   ☐ architect
   ☐ accountant
   ☐ teacher

2. Evelyn
   ☐ banker
   ☐ doctor
   ☐ lawyer

3. Edward
   ☐ marine biologist
   ☐ songwriter
   ☐ flight attendant

B Listen again. Write two reasons each person gives for his or her ideal job.

1. Alex _____
2. Evelyn _____
3. Edward _____

7 INTERCHANGE 10 You're hired.

Choose the right person for the job. Go to Interchange 10 on page 124.

8 WORD POWER Personality traits

A Which of these adjectives are positive (P)? Which are negative (N)?

creative	P	impatient
critical		level-headed
disorganized		moody
efficient		punctual
forgetful		reliable
generous		short-tempered
hardworking		strict

disorganized

hardworking

B **PAIR WORK** Tell your partner about people you know with these personality traits.

"My boss is very short-tempered. She often shouts at people . . ."

C Listen to four conversations. Then check (✓) the adjective that best describes each person.

1. a boss
   - ☐ creative
   - ☐ forgetful
   - ☐ serious

2. a co-worker
   - ☐ unfriendly
   - ☐ generous
   - ☐ strange

3. a teacher
   - ☐ moody
   - ☐ patient
   - ☐ hardworking

4. a relative
   - ☐ short-tempered
   - ☐ disorganized
   - ☐ reliable

9 PERSPECTIVES Making the right choice

A Listen to these people answer the question, "What kind of work would you like to do?" What job does each person talk about? Do they want that job?

Paula: "Well, I think I'd make a good journalist because I'm good at writing. When I was in high school, I worked as a reporter for the school website. I really enjoyed writing different kinds of articles."

Shawn: "I know what I *don't* want to do! A lot of my friends work in the stock market, but I could never be a stockbroker because I can't make decisions quickly. I don't mind working hard, but I'm terrible under pressure!"

Dalia: "I'm still in school. My parents want me to be a teacher, but I'm not sure yet. I guess I could be a teacher because I'm very creative. I'm also very impatient, so maybe I shouldn't work with kids."

B **PAIR WORK** Look at the interviews again. Who are you most like? least like? Why?

I like working with people. **67**

10 GRAMMAR FOCUS

▶ Clauses with *because*

The word *because* introduces a cause or reason.

I'd make a good journalist **because I'm good at writing**.
I could be a teacher **because I'm very creative**.
I wouldn't want to be a teacher **because I'm very impatient**.
I could never be a stockbroker **because I can't make decisions quickly**.

GRAMMAR PLUS see page 141

A Complete the sentences in column A with appropriate information from column B. Then compare with a partner.

A
1. I'd like to be a physical therapist ____
2. I would make a bad librarian ____
3. I couldn't be a diplomat ____
4. I wouldn't mind working as a veterinarian ____
5. I could be a flight attendant ____
6. I could never be a financial advisor ____

B
a. because I'm very disorganized.
b. because I love animals.
c. because I enjoy helping people.
d. because I'm not good at managing money.
e. because I'm short-tempered.
f. because I really enjoy traveling.

B GROUP WORK Think about your personal qualities and skills. Then complete these statements. Take turns discussing them with your group.

I could never be a . . . because . . .
I wouldn't mind working as a . . . because . . .
I'd make a good . . . because . . .
The best job for me is . . . because . . .

11 WRITING An online cover letter for a job application

A Imagine you are applying for one of the jobs in this unit. Write a short cover letter for a job application.

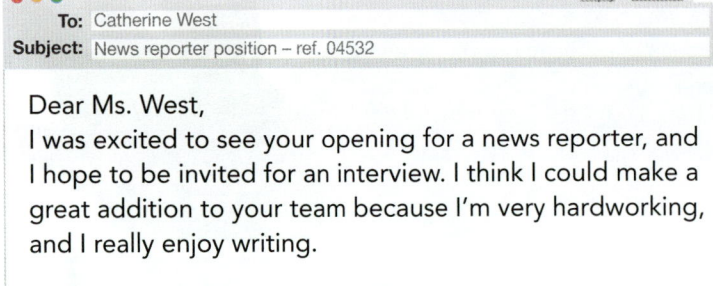

To: Catherine West
Subject: News reporter position – ref. 04532

Dear Ms. West,
I was excited to see your opening for a news reporter, and I hope to be invited for an interview. I think I could make a great addition to your team because I'm very hardworking, and I really enjoy writing.

As you can see from my résumé, I've had a lot of experience writing for my high school newspaper and for my college website. I also worked . . .

B PAIR WORK Exchange papers. If you received this cover letter, would you invite the applicant for a job interview? Why or why not?

12 READING

A Skim the advertisement. Which three cross-cultural problems does it mention?

GLOBAL WORK SOLUTIONS

At GW Solutions, we recognize the importance of cross-cultural training for U.S. employees working abroad. Lack of cultural understanding results in lost contracts and less business. Here are some examples of what our courses can teach you.

In the U.S.A., we say that time is money. For American workers, punctuality and timetables are always important. At work, people concentrate on the task they are doing. They usually do not spend a lot of time on small talk. However, it's important to realize that not all cultures see time in this way. In many African countries, for example, getting work done isn't the only valuable use of time. Spending time at work to build close relationships with colleagues is equally important. It's important to ask about your colleague's personal life. Understanding these cultural differences is essential for working in a global team. If an American doesn't realize this, he or she might think that an African colleague who spends a lot of time chatting with co-workers is being lazy or avoiding doing his or her work. And an African worker might think their American colleague is the rudest person they've ever met!

In the U.S.A., written agreements are essential. Business deals are always agreed through a contract and once it has been signed, we consider it to be final. The conditions of the agreement don't usually change without the signing of another contract. But you may do business in places where this is not the case. In China, for example, people generally place more trust in a person's word than in a signed contract. Once a good relationship exists, a simple handshake might be enough to reach a business deal.

In the U.S.A., workers generally speak directly, and they openly disagree with colleagues. This kind of "straight talk" is seen as a mark of honesty. But where we see honesty, others may see rudeness. In some parts of Asia, open disagreement with colleagues may not be acceptable because it makes people feel embarrassed. Instead, you should stop and think for a while. Afterward you could say, "I agree in general, but could a different idea work in this situation?" And your body language is important, too. In the West, direct eye contact is good because it's a sign of honesty. In some Asian cultures, it's polite to avoid looking directly at your colleagues in order to show respect.

Did you learn something new? Need to know more? Sign up for one of our training courses and learn how to do business wherever you go.

B Read the advertisement. Then correct the sentences.
1. Ideas about work time are the same in Africa and the U.S.A.
2. Written contracts are more important in China than in the U.S.A.
3. American and Asian workers have similar ways of communicating.

C Complete these sentences with words from the advertisement.
1. In the U.S.A., being _____ is very important at work.
2. African workers like to have strong _____ with their co-workers.
3. In China, people might agree to a business deal with a _____.
4. For Americans, it's normal to _____ openly when they have a different opinion.
5. Some workers _____ making eye contact when talking to others.

D Look at the sentences in part C. Are they true for your country? What advice would you give to a foreigner coming to work in your country?

I like working with people.

Units 9–10 Progress check

SELF-ASSESSMENT

How well can you do these things? Check (✓) the boxes.

I can . . .	Very well	OK	A little
Describe people and things in the past, present, and future (Ex. 1)	☐	☐	☐
Discuss possible consequences of actions (Ex. 2)	☐	☐	☐
Understand descriptions of skills and personality traits (Ex. 3, 4)	☐	☐	☐
Discuss job skills (Ex. 4)	☐	☐	☐
Give reasons for my opinions (Ex. 4)	☐	☐	☐

1 SPEAKING Things have changed.

A PAIR WORK Think of one more question for each category. Then interview a partner.

Free time How did you spend your free time as a child? What do you like to do these days? How are you going to spend your free time next year?

Friends Who used to be your friends when you were a kid? How do you meet new people nowadays? How do you think people will meet in the future?

B GROUP WORK Share one interesting thing about your partner.

2 GAME Share the consequences

A Add two situations and two consequences to the lists below.

Situation
- ☐ you spend too much time online
- ☐ you get a well-paid job
- ☐ you move to a foreign country
- ☐ it's sunny tomorrow
- ☐ you don't study hard
- ☐ you fall in love
- ☐ _____
- ☐ _____

Consequences
- ☐ learn about a different culture
- ☐ get good grades
- ☐ buy an expensive car
- ☐ feel jealous sometimes
- ☐ go to the beach
- ☐ have time for your family and friends
- ☐ _____
- ☐ _____

B CLASS ACTIVITY Go around the class and make sentences. Check (✓) each *if* clause after you use it. The student who uses the most clauses correctly wins.

"If you spend too much time online, you won't . . ."

3 LISTENING What do you want to do?

A Listen to Michelle and Robbie discuss four jobs. Write down the jobs and check (✓) if they would be good or bad at them.

	Job	Good	Bad	Reason
1. Michelle		☐ ☐	☐ ☐	
2. Robbie		☐ ☐	☐ ☐	

B Listen again. Write down the reasons they give.

C PAIR WORK Look at the jobs from part A. Which ones would you be good at? Why?

4 DISCUSSION Job profile

A Prepare a personal job profile. Write your name, skills, and job preferences. Think about the questions below. Then compare with a partner.

Do you . . . ?
enjoy helping people
have any special skills
have any experience
have a good memory

Are you good at . . . ?
communicating with people
solving problems
making decisions quickly
learning foreign languages

Do you mind . . . ?
wearing a uniform
traveling frequently
working with a team
working long hours

A: Do you enjoy helping people?
B: Sure. I often do volunteer work.
A: So do I. I help at our local . . .

B GROUP WORK Make suggestions for possible jobs based on your classmates' job profiles. Give reasons for your opinions. What do you think of their suggestions for you?

A: Victor would be a good psychologist because he's good at communicating with people.
B: No way! I could never be a psychologist. I'm very moody and short-tempered!

WHAT'S NEXT?

Look at your Self-assessment again. Do you need to review anything?

Units 9–10 Progress check

11 It's really worth seeing!

▸ Discuss famous landmarks, monuments, and works of art
▸ Discuss countries around the world

1 SNAPSHOT

AMAZING FACTS ABOUT AMAZING LANDMARKS

The Eiffel Tower – When it was opened in 1889, the tower was red. After a decade, it was painted yellow, and later, it was covered in different shades of brown.

Machu Picchu – It is located 2,430 m (7,972 ft) above sea level, and it has resisted several earthquakes. When there is an earthquake, the stones "dance" and fall back into place.

The Neuschwanstein Castle – This beautiful castle in Germany was the inspiration for the Walt Disney Magic Kingdom Sleeping Beauty Castle.

Mount Fuji – The highest mountain in Japan is made up of a few volcanoes. The last recorded eruption started in 1707.

The Statue of Liberty – The 350 pieces were made in France and then shipped to the United States.

Big Ben – The tower is named Elizabeth Tower. Big Ben is the name of the bell inside it.

Did you know these facts about the landmarks above? What else do you know about them?
Have you ever visited any of them? Which would you like to visit? Why?
Do you know any interesting facts about landmarks in your country?

2 PERSPECTIVES Where dreams come true

A How much do you know about the Walt Disney Company and theme parks?
Find three mistakes in the statements below. Then listen and check your answers.

1. The Walt Disney Company was founded in 1923 in California by Walt Disney and his brother Roy.
2. Their most famous character, Donald Duck, first appeared in a movie in 1928.
3. The first Disney theme park, Disneyland, was opened in 1955 in New York and soon became an international attraction.
4. The official opening was broadcast live by the ABC television network.
5. In 1971, the company opened their second park, Disney World.
6. Some of their most popular parks in Florida include Magic Kingdom, Animal Kingdom, and Epcot Center.
7. In 1983, the company opened their first foreign park, London Disneyland. Later, theme parks were also opened in Paris, Hong Kong, and Shanghai.

B GROUP WORK Have you been to a Disney park? Which one?
How did you like it? Which one would you like to go to? Why?

3 GRAMMAR FOCUS

▶ Passive with *by* (simple past)

The passive changes the focus of a sentence.
For the simple past, use the past of *be* + past participle.

Active	Passive
The Disney brothers **founded** the company in 1923.	It **was founded by** the Disney brothers in 1923.
Walt Disney **opened** Disneyland in 1955.	Disneyland **was opened by** Walt Disney in 1955.
The ABC network **broadcast** the opening of the park.	The opening **was broadcast by** ABC.

GRAMMAR PLUS see page 142

A Complete the sentences with the simple past passive form of the verbs. Then compare with a partner.

1. *Mont Sainte-Victoire* _____ (paint) by the French artist Paul Cézanne.
2. The first Star Wars film _____ (write) and _____ (direct) by George Lucas.
3. The Statue of Liberty _____ (design) by the French sculptor Frédéric Auguste Bartholdi.
4. The 2014 World Cup final _____ (win) by Germany. The final match _____ (see) by almost 1 billion people all over the world.
5. The songs *Revolution* and *Hey Jude* _____ (record) by the Beatles in 1968.
6. In the 2007 film *I'm Not There*, the American musician Bob Dylan _____ (play) by six different people, including Australian actress Cate Blanchett.
7. The 2016 Oscar for Best Actress _____ (give) to Brie Larson for her role in the movie *Room*.
8. The first iPad _____ (release) in 2010.

B PAIR WORK Change these sentences into passive sentences with *by*.
Then take turns reading them aloud.

1. Eddie Redmayne played Stephen Hawking in the 2014 film *The Theory of Everything*.
   _____
2. Gabriel García Márquez wrote the novel *One Hundred Years of Solitude* in 1967.
   _____
3. The American architect William Lamb designed the Empire State Building.
   _____
4. Woo Paik produced the first digital HDTV in 1991.
   _____
5. J. K. Rowling wrote the first Harry Potter book on an old manual typewriter.
   _____
6. *Empire* magazine readers chose Indiana Jones as the greatest movie character of all time.
   _____

4 INTERCHANGE 11 True or false?

Who created these well-known works? Go to Interchange 11 on page 125.

It's really worth seeing! **73**

5 PRONUNCIATION The letter o

A Listen and practice. Notice how the letter o is pronounced in the following words.

/a/	/ou/	/u/	/ʌ/
not	no	do	one
top	don't	food	love
_____	_____	_____	_____
_____	_____	_____	_____

B How is the letter o pronounced in these words? Write them in the correct column in part A. Then listen and check your answers.

come   done   lock   own   shot   soon   who   wrote

6 LISTENING Man-made wonders of the world

A Listen to three tour guides describe some famous monuments. Take notes to answer the questions below. Then compare with a partner.

1. Taj Mahal
Why was it built?
What do the changing colors of the building represent?

2. Palace of Versailles
What did King Louis XIV want the Hall of Mirrors to show?
What problem did the candles cause? How did the mirrors help?

3. La Sagrada Familia
What did the architect think about man-made structures versus nature?
Why are no straight lines used?

B **PAIR WORK** Think of another famous monument. Describe it to the rest of the class. They will try to guess the monument.

7 WORD POWER Country fast facts

A Complete the sentences with words from the list.

✓ cattle	dialects	electronics	handicrafts	languages
sheep	souvenirs	✓ soybeans	textiles	wheat

1. The United States **grows** ___soybeans___ and _____.
2. Australia **raises** ___cattle___ and _____.
3. China **manufactures** _____ and _____.
4. In India, people **speak** many different _____ and _____.
5. You can **find** _____ and _____ at different shops in Brazil.

B **PAIR WORK** Talk about your country. Use the sentences in part A with your own information.
"We raise cattle and chickens. We grow corn and oats. You can find . . ."

8 CONVERSATION What do you want to know?

A Listen and practice.

Lisa: Erik, you're from Amsterdam, aren't you?
Erik: Yeah . . . Why?
Lisa: I'm going there for a conference, and I'd like some information.
Erik: Sure. What do you want to know?
Lisa: Do you use the euro in the Netherlands?
Erik: Yes. The euro is used in most of Europe, you know.
Lisa: And do I need to take euros with me?
Erik: Not really. International credit cards are accepted everywhere, and they're much safer.
Lisa: Of course. And what should I buy there?
Erik: Cheese, definitely. We raise dairy cows, and some really excellent cheese is made from their milk.
Lisa: Good. I love cheese. Where is it sold?
Erik: You can find it at cheese shops all around the city. And don't forget to bring me a piece.

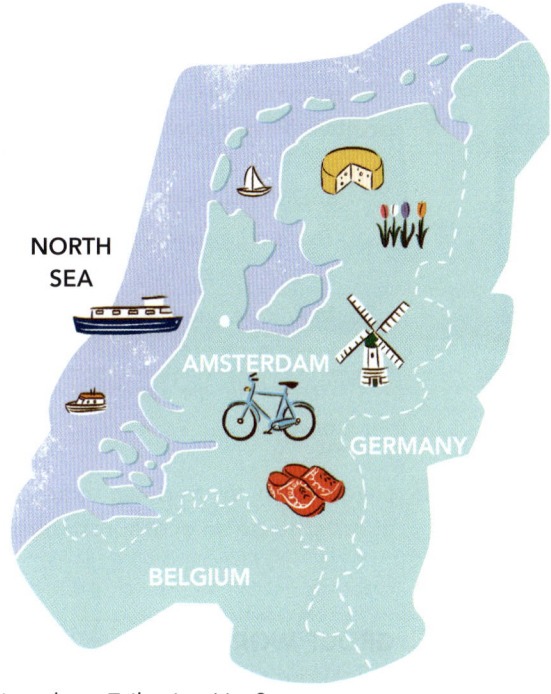

B Listen to the rest of the conversation. What other suggestion does Erik give Lisa?

9 GRAMMAR FOCUS

> **Passive without *by* (simple present)**
>
> **For the simple present, use the present of *be* + past participle.**
>
> | Active | Passive |
> |---|---|
> | They **use** the euro in most of Europe. | The euro **is used** in most of Europe. |
> | Most places **accept** credit cards. | Credit cards **are accepted** at most places. |
> | We **raise** dairy cattle in the Netherlands. | Dairy cattle **are raised** in the Netherlands. |
>
> **GRAMMAR PLUS** see page 142

A Complete the sentences. Use the passive of these verbs.

| grow | manufacture | raise | speak | sell | use |

1. French and Flemish _____ in Belgium.
2. Rice _____ in many Asian countries.
3. Cars and electronics _____ in Japan.
4. Sheep's milk _____ for making feta cheese.
5. Handicrafts _____ in the streets in Thailand.
6. A lot of cattle _____ in Australia.

B Complete this passage using the simple present passive form.

Many crops _____ (grow) in Taiwan. Some crops _____ (consume) locally, but others _____ (export). Tea _____ (grow) in cooler parts of the island, and rice _____ (cultivate) in warmer parts. Fishing is also an important industry. A wide variety of seafood _____ (catch) and _____ (ship) all over the world. Many people _____ (employ) in the food-processing industry.

C **PAIR WORK** Use the passive of the verbs in part A to talk about your country and other countries you know.

It's really worth seeing! 75

10 LISTENING Is all tourism good?

A Listen to a news report about tourism in Costa Rica. Select the six effects of mass tourism that are mentioned. (There are two extra effects.) Indicate if they are positive (**P**) or negative (**N**).

Costa Rica

P	English is spoken.	The ocean is polluted.
	Tourism jobs are available all over the country.	High-rise hotels are built.
	More foreigners are investing there.	Fish and lobster are hunted.
	Acres of jungle are cut down.	The government becomes corrupt.

B Listen again. Write down three criteria the hotel fulfills in order to be an ecotourism business in Costa Rica.

_____   _____   _____

C GROUP WORK What is tourism like in your country? Talk about some positive and negative aspects.

11 SPEAKING Give me a clue.

A PAIR WORK Choose a country. Then answer these questions.

Where is it located?
What traditional dishes are eaten there?
What languages are spoken?
What currency is used?
What famous tourist attraction is found there?
What souvenirs are found there?

B CLASS ACTIVITY Give a short talk about the country you chose. Don't say the country's name. Can the class guess the country?

12 WRITING A city guide

A Choose a city or area in your country and write the introduction for an online city guide. Include the location, size, population, main attractions, shopping and travel tips, etc.

> Bruges is located in the northwest of Belgium, and it has a population of about 120,000 people. It is known for its canals and medieval buildings. In 2000, it was declared a World Heritage City by UNESCO. Bruges is also a good place to buy Belgium chocolate. It is sold . . .

Bruges, Belgium

B GROUP WORK Exchange papers. Do you think the introduction gives a good idea of the place? Would it attract tourists or businesses to the place? What other information should be included?

13 READING

A Scan the advertisements. How many types of toilets can you see at the museum? When were the underwater sculptures designed? How big is the world's smallest book?

A SULABH INTERNATIONAL MUSEUM OF TOILETS, NEW DELHI, INDIA

Ever wondered about the history of toilets? Probably not! But visit the fascinating Sulabh Museum and see just how interesting they can be. Admire nearly 300 different toilets dating back to 2500 B.C.E. Some are beautifully decorated, one is made of solid gold, and there is an electric toilet that works without water. The star of the collection is a copy of a 16th century toilet. It was used by King Louis XIV of France – sometimes while speaking to his government. See drawings, photographs, and poems about toilets, too. One photo shows a toilet that was used by an elephant!

B UNDERWATER MUSEUM, CANCUN, MEXICO

Join one of our unique tours and discover an amazing underwater world 27 feet below the sea. Designed by Jason deCaires Taylor in 2009, it has over 450 sculptures. They are made from natural materials and show art and nature existing side by side. The *Silent Evolution* shows men, women, and children standing together on the seabed. They look so real that you'll want to talk to them. There are also sculptures of a house and a life-size Beetle car. The sculptures are covered in beautiful corals, and their appearances are constantly changing. Watch as an incredible variety of fish swim in and out of them.

C MICROMINIATURE MUSEUM, KIEV, UKRAINE

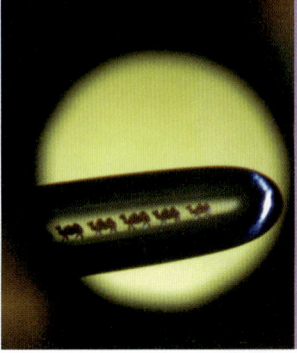

Small really is beautiful in this museum of art with a difference. The exhibits, created by artist Nikolai Syadristy, are so tiny they can only be seen clearly with a microscope. Read the world's smallest book – it is only 0.6 millimeters in size, but contains twelve pages of poems and drawings. There is a chess set on the head of a pin and the world's smallest electric motor. It is 20 times smaller than a piece of sand. Look closely at the eye of a needle and discover the seven camels inside. Read the words "Long Live Peace" not on paper, but written on a human hair!

B Read the advertisements. Find the words in *italics* below. Then circle the meaning of each word.

1. Something *fascinating* makes you feel very **interested / angry**.
2. The *star* of a collection is the **worst / best** part.
3. A *unique* thing is **different from / the same as** all others.
4. If something is changing *constantly*, it's changing **very little / all the time**.
5. An *exhibit* is an object that is **on show / for sale**.
6. A *needle* is a metal object that is used for **cutting / sewing**.

C Read the comments of three visitors to the museums. Write the letter (A, B, or C) of the museum you think they visited.

_____ 1. "I just don't know how he made such little things."
_____ 2. "I can't believe that an animal would use something like that."
_____ 3. "I felt a little afraid about going down, but it was a great experience in the end."

D Which museum would you most like to visit? Why?

It's really worth seeing!

12 It's a long story.

▸ Tell stories
▸ Discuss recent activities

1 SNAPSHOT

True Stories of Incredible Coincidences

One day, the American novelist Anne Parrish was in a bookstore in Paris and she saw an old, used copy of one of her favorite childhood books. When she opened it, she saw on the first page: "Anne Parrish, 209 N. Weber Street, Colorado Springs." It was Anne's own book.

A 10-year-old girl named Laura Buxton released a bunch of balloons into the air. She attached a note to the balloons that asked the person who found it to write back to her. A couple of weeks later, she received a reply. It was from another 10-year-old girl also named Laura Buxton who lived 150 miles away.

Which of these stories do you think is more amazing? more difficult to believe?
Have you ever had an experience that is hard to believe?
Do you know of anyone who has? What happened?

2 PERSPECTIVES What next?

A Listen to what happened to these people. Check (✓) the things that have happened to you.

- ☐ "I was having lunch when I spilled a cup of coffee on my clothes."
- ☐ "I was driving to the airport to pick up a friend, but I got a flat tire."
- ☐ "I was studying for an important test when the lights went out."
- ☐ "While I was walking down the street, I found a wallet with lots of money."
- ☐ "I was traveling in another country when I met an old school friend."
- ☐ "I was getting off a bus when I slipped and fell on the sidewalk."
- ☐ "While I was shopping one day, a celebrity walked into the store."

B Choose one statement that you checked. What happened next?

"I tried to clean it, but I couldn't. So I had to wear a jacket for the rest of the day."

78

3 GRAMMAR FOCUS

Past continuous vs. simple past

Use the past continuous for an action in progress in the past.
Use the simple past for an action that interrupts it.

I **was having** lunch	when I **spilled** coffee on my clothes.
I **was driving** to the airport,	but I **got** a flat tire.
While I **was shopping** one day,	a celebrity **walked** into the store.

GRAMMAR PLUS see page 143

A Complete these sentences. Then compare with a partner.

1. My sister _____ (text) while she _____ (drive), and she almost _____ (crash) her car.
2. While I _____ (cook) dinner last night, a friend _____ (call) and I _____ (burn) the food.
3. My father _____ (ski) when he _____ (break) his leg in several places.
4. We _____ (have) our first child while we _____ (live) in a tiny apartment.
5. While I _____ (drive) in England a few years ago, I _____ (realize) I was on the wrong side of the road!
6. Once I _____ (read) a good book, but someone _____ (tell) me the ending.
7. My parents _____ (meet) each other while they _____ (work) at the same restaurant in Vancouver.

B Complete these statements with information about yourself. Use the simple past or the past continuous.

1. I was taking a selfie when . . .
2. While I was going home one day, . . .
3. I was . . .
4. While I was . . .
5. Last month, . . .
6. Some time ago, . . .

C **PAIR WORK** Take turns reading your sentences from part B. Then ask and answer follow-up questions.

A: I was taking a selfie when a man came and stole my phone.
B: Oh, no! What did you do?
A: I went to the police . . . and they told me to be more careful.

It's a long story.

4 LISTENING How did it all begin?

A Listen to this story about a successful inventor. Put the sentences into the correct order from 1 to 8.

_1_ Mark Zuckerberg started writing computer programs.
___ His friends invested in Facebook.
___ He didn't accept Microsoft's offer.
___ He invented FaceMash.
___ Facebook became available to the public.
___ Zuckerberg wrote his very own messenger program.
___ He created a program that recommended music.
___ Three classmates asked for his help.

B Listen again. How did the invention change his life?

C PAIR WORK Think of other websites and apps that were successful inventions.

5 WORD POWER What happened?

A Some adverbs are often used in storytelling to emphasize that something interesting is about to happen. Which of these adverbs are positive (**P**)? Which are negative (**N**)? Which could be either (**E**)?

coincidentally ___	strangely ___
fortunately ___	suddenly ___
luckily ___	surprisingly ___
miraculously ___	unexpectedly ___
sadly ___	unfortunately ___

B PAIR WORK Complete these statements with adverbs from part A to make up creative sentences.

We were having a party when, . . .
I was walking down the street when, . . .
It started out as a normal day, but, . . .

A: We were having a party when, suddenly, the lights went out!
B: Once I was dancing at a party when, unfortunately, I fell down!

6 WRITING What's your story?

A Write a short story about something that happened to you recently. Try to include some of the adverbs from Exercise 5.

> I was shopping at a big department store when, suddenly, I saw a little girl crying in a corner all by herself. The girl said she couldn't find her mother. I was taking her to the store manager when I saw an old school friend running towards me. Coincidentally, she was the girl's mother, and . . .

B GROUP WORK Take turns reading your stories. Answer any questions from the group.

7 CONVERSATION What have you been doing?

A Listen and practice.

Steve: Hey, Luiza! I haven't seen you in ages. What have you been doing lately?
Luiza: I haven't been going out much. I've been working two jobs for the last six months.
Steve: How come?
Luiza: I'm saving up money for a trip to Morocco.
Steve: Well, that's exciting!
Luiza: Yeah, it is. What about you?
Steve: Well, I've only been *spending* money. I've been trying to become an actor. I've been taking courses and going to a lot of auditions.
Luiza: Really? How long have you been trying?
Steve: Since I graduated. But I haven't had any luck yet. No one recognizes my talent.

B Listen to two other people at the party. What has happened since they last saw each other?

8 GRAMMAR FOCUS

Present perfect continuous

Use the present perfect continuous for actions that start in the past and continue into the present.

What **have** you **been doing** lately?
How long **have** you **been trying**?
Have you **been saving** money?

I've been working two jobs for the last six months.
I've been trying since I graduated.
No, **I haven't been saving** money. **I've been spending** it!

GRAMMAR PLUS see page 143

A Complete the conversations with the present perfect continuous.

1. **A:** _____ you _____ (learn) any new skills this year?
   B: Yes, I have. I _____ (take) some art courses.
2. **A:** What _____ you _____ (do) lately?
   B: Well, I _____ (look for) a new job.
3. **A:** How _____ you _____ (feel) recently?
   B: Great! I _____ (run) three times a week. And I _____ (not drink) as much coffee since I stopped working at the coffee shop.
4. **A:** _____ you _____ (get) enough exercise lately?
   B: No, I haven't. I _____ (study) a lot for a big exam.

B **PAIR WORK** Read the conversations in part A together. Then read them again and answer the questions with your own information.

A: Have you been learning any new skills this year?
B: Yes, I've been taking guitar lessons.

It's a long story. 81

9 PRONUNCIATION Contrastive stress in responses

A Listen and practice. Notice how the stress changes to emphasize a contrast.

A: Has your brother been studying German?
B: No, I've been studying German.

A: Have you been teaching French?
B: No, I've been studying French.

B Mark the stress changes in these conversations. Listen and check. Then practice the conversations.

A: Have you been studying for ten years?
B: No, I've been studying for two years.

A: Have you been studying at school?
B: No, I've been studying at home.

10 SPEAKING Tell me about it.

GROUP WORK Add three questions to this list. Then take turns asking and answering the questions. Remember to ask for further information.

Have you been . . . lately?
traveling
watching any good TV series
taking any lessons
working out
working long hours
going out a lot
staying up late

_____
_____
_____

useful expressions
Really?
I didn't know that!
Oh, I see.
I had no idea.
Wow! Tell me more.

A: Have you been traveling lately?
B: Yes, I have. I've been going abroad about once a month.
C: Really? Lucky you!
B: Not exactly. I've been traveling for work, not on vacation.

11 INTERCHANGE 12 It's my life.

Play a board game. Go to Interchange 12 on page 126.

12 READING

A Skim the article. What is special about these musicians? How have they influenced other people?

BREAKING DOWN THE SOUND OF SILENCE

Ten years before he died, the composer Beethoven went deaf. He called this disability his "nightmare." Fortunately for thousands of classical music fans, he didn't stop writing brilliant music. One hundred and eighty years later, being deaf hasn't stopped three Americans – Steve Longo, Ed Chevy, and Bob Hiltermann – from playing music, either. In their case, the music is rock, and their band is called Beethoven's Nightmare.

The three boys grew up in different cities, but they all showed a surprising interest in music. Although they couldn't hear it, they were amazed by the energy of 1960s bands like the Beatles. They could see the effect the music had on the audiences – the happy faces of friends and family as they watched. Something exciting was obviously happening. "I'm going to do that, too," they all said. "Why? You can't hear," asked parents, teachers, and friends alike. Each boy used sign language to answer, "Because I can feel it."

Longo and Chevy started playing the guitar. They put on headphones and turned up the volume. With the help of powerful hearing aids, they could get some of the notes – the rest they felt through vibrations. Drummer Hiltermann came from a musical family. His parents thought that teaching their son to play an instrument was a waste of time. But they changed their minds after he nearly drove them crazy by using knives and forks to drum on the furniture of the house.

The three men first met in college in Washington, D.C. They started a band and played many concerts until they graduated in 1975. In 2001, Hiltermann had the idea to bring his old friends together again. They have been performing ever since. In 2013, a new member, Paul Raci, joined the band as a singer. At concerts, dancers put on a spectacular show and use sign language to explain the words of the songs to the audience. And, of course, the band plays very loudly!

The group has encouraged many deaf people, and people with other disabilities, to follow their dreams. Chevy says, "The only thing deaf people *can't* do is hear."

Dennis McCarthy, "Deaf band 'Beethoven's Nightmare' feels the music," *Los Angeles Daily News* (Oct. 31, 2013). Used with permission.

B Read the article. Choose the correct word(s) in the sentences below.
1. After going deaf, Beethoven **continued / refused** to compose music.
2. The boys knew music was powerful because of something they **read / saw**.
3. Many people didn't **understand / like** the boys' ambition to play music.
4. Hiltermann's parents **wanted / didn't want** him to learn to play at first.
5. The three young men started playing together **before / after** finishing college.

C Answer the questions.
1. Which band inspired the three boys to play music?
2. What did Longo and Chevy use to hear some parts of the music?
3. What did Hiltermann use to make noise in his house?
4. Where did the three men get to know each other?
5. When did Beethoven's Nightmare start playing?

D Do you think it's very difficult for people in your country to achieve their dreams? What new technology and facilities make it easier for them?

It's a long story.

Units 11–12 Progress check

SELF-ASSESSMENT

How well can you do these things? Check (✓) the boxes.

I can . . .	Very well	OK	A little
Give information about books, movies, songs, etc. (Ex. 1)	☐	☐	☐
Understand information about countries (Ex. 2)	☐	☐	☐
Describe a situation (Ex. 3)	☐	☐	☐
Ask and answer questions about past events (Ex. 4, 5)	☐	☐	☐
Ask and answer questions about recent activities (Ex. 5)	☐	☐	☐

1 SPEAKING Trivia questions

A List six books, movies, songs, albums, or other popular works. Then write one *who* question for each of the six items.

> Harry Potter books
> Who wrote the Harry Potter books?

B **PAIR WORK** Take turns asking your questions. Use the passive with *by* to answer.

A: Who wrote the *Harry Potter* books?
B: I think they were written by J. K. Rowling.

2 LISTENING Did you know?

A Listen to a game show about Spain. Write the correct answers.

1. How many languages are officially recognized? _____
2. What day is considered bad luck? _____
3. What is the most valuable soccer team in the world? _____
4. In how many countries is Spanish the official language? _____
5. What fruit is thrown at the world's biggest food fight? _____
6. What is Spain's famous dance called? _____

B Listen again. Keep score. How much money does each contestant have?

3 GAME What happened?

GROUP WORK Use the passive to write details about these situations. Then compare with the class. Which group wrote the most sentences?

The lights went out.
Our class was canceled.

It snowed a lot yesterday.
Many roads were blocked.

Your roommate cleaned the apartment.
The dishes were done.

4 ROLE PLAY Do you have an alibi?

A famous painting has been stolen from a local museum. It disappeared last Sunday afternoon between 12:00 P.M. and 4:00 P.M.

Student A: Student B suspects you stole the painting. Make up an alibi. Take notes on what you were doing that day. Then answer Student B's questions.

Student B: You are a police detective. You think Student A stole the painting. Add two questions to the notebook. Then ask Student A the questions.

Where were you last Sunday?
Where did you go for lunch?
Did anyone see you?
What were you wearing that day?
What were you doing between noon and 4:00 P.M.?
Was anyone with you?
_____
_____

Change roles and try the role play again.

5 DISCUSSION Is that so?

A GROUP WORK What interesting things can you find out about your classmates? Ask these questions and others of your own.

Have you been doing anything exciting recently?
Where do you live? How long have you been living there?
Have you met anyone interesting lately?
Who is your best friend? How did you meet? How long have you been friends?
Where were you living ten years ago? Did you like it there? What do you remember about it?

useful expressions

Really?
I didn't know that!
Oh, I see.
I had no idea.
Wow! Tell me more.

B CLASS ACTIVITY Tell the class the most interesting thing you learned.

WHAT'S NEXT?

Look at your Self-assessment again. Do you need to review anything?

13 That's entertainment!

▶ Discuss popular entertainment
▶ Discuss movies and famous Hollywood names

1 SNAPSHOT

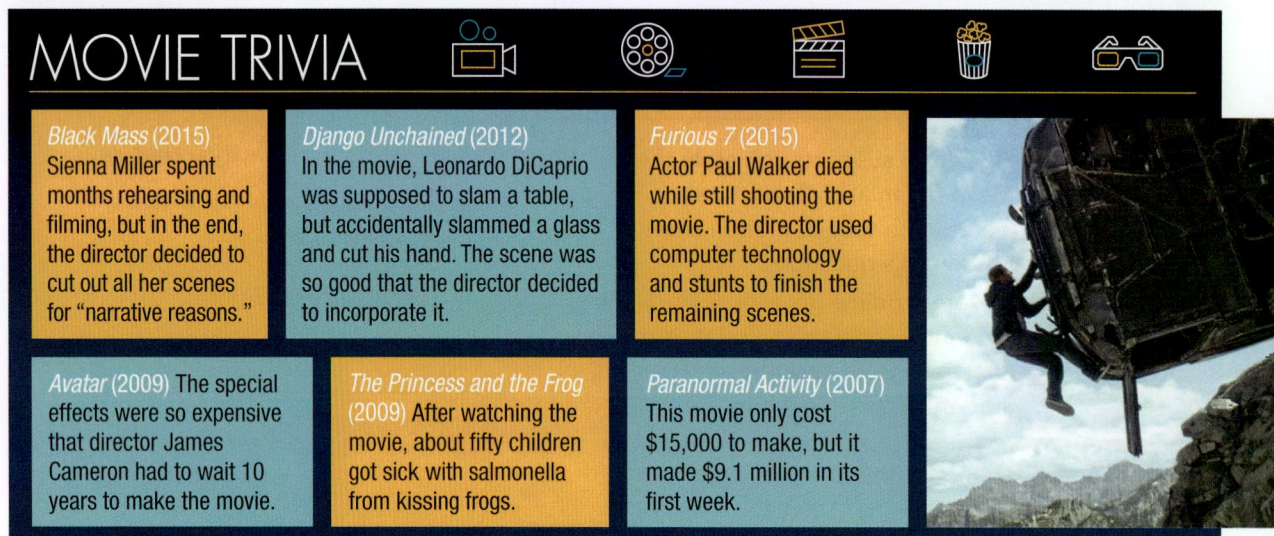

MOVIE TRIVIA

Black Mass (2015)
Sienna Miller spent months rehearsing and filming, but in the end, the director decided to cut out all her scenes for "narrative reasons."

Django Unchained (2012)
In the movie, Leonardo DiCaprio was supposed to slam a table, but accidentally slammed a glass and cut his hand. The scene was so good that the director decided to incorporate it.

Furious 7 (2015)
Actor Paul Walker died while still shooting the movie. The director used computer technology and stunts to finish the remaining scenes.

Avatar (2009) The special effects were so expensive that director James Cameron had to wait 10 years to make the movie.

The Princess and the Frog (2009) After watching the movie, about fifty children got sick with salmonella from kissing frogs.

Paranormal Activity (2007) This movie only cost $15,000 to make, but it made $9.1 million in its first week.

Which of the movie trivia do you find most interesting?
Do you know any other movie trivia?
Which of these movies have you seen? Did you enjoy it? Which would you like to watch?

2 CONVERSATION I think they're boring.

A Listen and practice.

Danny: It's so hot out. Do you want to stay in and watch a movie this afternoon?
Gina: Hmm. Maybe. What do you want to see?
Danny: How about an *X-Men* movie? I've heard that the early ones are really interesting.
Gina: For you, maybe. I'm not interested in action movies. Actually, I think they're boring.
Danny: What about that new movie based on one of Stephen King's novels?
Gina: I don't know. I'm always fascinated by his books, but I'm not in the mood for a horror movie.
Danny: Well, what do you want to see?
Gina: How about a *Game of Thrones* marathon? It's my favorite series ever.
Danny: OK, but only if you make us some popcorn.

B Listen to the rest of the conversation. What happens next? What do they decide to do?

3 GRAMMAR FOCUS

Participles as adjectives

Present participles
That *X-Men* movie sounds **interesting**.
Stephen King's books are **fascinating**.
I think action movies are **boring**.

Past participles
I'm not **interested** in action movies.
I'm **fascinated** by Stephen King's books.
I'm **bored** by action movies.

GRAMMAR PLUS see page 144

A Complete these sentences. Then compare with a partner.

1. John Cho is such an _____ actor. I'm always _____ by his incredible talent. (amaze)
2. Most TV shows are really _____. I often get so _____ watching them that I fall asleep. (bore)
3. I was _____ in watching *The Martian* after I read the book. And I was surprised that the movie is really _____. (interest)
4. I'm _____ to watch *The Avengers*. Everybody has told me it's really _____. (excite)
5. I find animated films very _____. I've been _____ by them since I was a little kid. (amuse / fascinate)
6. It's _____ that horror movies are so popular. I can't understand why people go to the movies to feel _____. (surprise / terrify)

John Cho

B **PAIR WORK** Complete the description below with the correct forms of the words.

| amaze | annoy | confuse | disgust | embarrass | shock |

I had a terrible time at the movies last weekend. First, my ticket cost $25. I was really _____ by the price. By mistake, I gave the cashier two $5 bills instead of a twenty and a five. I was a little _____. Then there was trash all over the theater. The mess was _____. The people behind me were talking during the movie, which was _____. The story was hard to follow. I always find thrillers so _____. I liked the special effects, though. They were _____!

4 WORD POWER How do you like it?

A **PAIR WORK** Complete the chart with synonyms from the list.

amusing	dumb	horrible	odd	silly
bizarre	fantastic	hysterical	outstanding	terrible
disgusting	hilarious	incredible	ridiculous	weird

Awful	Wonderful	Stupid	Strange	Funny

B **GROUP WORK** Share your opinions about a movie, an actor, an actress, a TV show, and a book. Use words from part A.

That's entertainment! **87**

5 LISTENING What did you think?

A Listen to people talk about books, movies, and TV programs. Match each conversation to the statement that best describes the people's opinions.

1. ____   a. This special offers an amazing look into an exotic country.
2. ____   b. The new investigation into these creatures was a waste of time.
3. ____   c. The bad acting with this boring idea makes it terrible.
4. ____   d. She is excited to read more of this clever mystery series.

B Listen again. Write a reason each person gives to support his or her opinion.

1. _____   3. _____
2. _____   4. _____

6 PRONUNCIATION Emphatic stress

A Listen and practice. Notice how stress and a higher pitch are used to express strong opinions.

That was terrible!   He was amazing!   That's fascinating!

B PAIR WORK Write four statements using these words. Then take turns reading them. Pay attention to emphatic stress.

fantastic   horrible   ridiculous   weird

7 DISCUSSION I give it two thumbs up!

A PAIR WORK Take turns asking and answering these questions and others of your own.

What kinds of movies are you interested in? Why?
What kinds of movies do you find boring?
Who are your favorite actors and actresses? Why?
Are there actors or actresses you don't like?
What's the worst movie you've ever seen?
Are there any outstanding movies playing now?
Do you prefer to watch films dubbed or with subtitles? Why?

A: What kinds of movies are you interested in?
B: I like romantic comedies.
A: Really? Why is that?
B: They're entertaining! What about you?
A: I think romantic comedies are kind of dumb. I prefer . . .

B GROUP WORK Compare your information. Whose taste in movies is most like yours?

Action
Comedy
Animation
Fantasy
Biography
Sci-Fi
Thriller
Horror
Drama
War
Documentary

8 PERSPECTIVES And the Oscar goes to . . .

A Listen to people talk about some of their Hollywood favorites. Can you guess the actress, actor, or movie each person is describing?

1. He's a famous American actor who is also a successful director and producer. He won the Oscar for Best Motion Picture in 2013 with *Argo*, which he directed and co-produced.
2. The first movie in the series came out in 1977. It's a science fiction fantasy that has become a blockbuster franchise. The story takes place "a long time ago in a galaxy far, far away."
3. I really like animated movies, and the third one in this series is my favorite. It's about a boy's toys that have a secret life full of adventures when they are alone.
4. She's an actress that is excellent in both dramas and comedies. I loved her in *Mamma Mia!* and *The Devil Wears Prada*. In 2011, she won her third Oscar for her performance in *The Iron Lady*.

B Do you like the people and movies described in part A? What else do you know about them?

9 GRAMMAR FOCUS

Relative pronouns for people and things

Use *who* or *that* for people.
He's an actor. He's also a director and producer.
He's an actor **who/that** is also a director and producer.

Use *which* or *that* for things.
It's a science fiction fantasy. It has become a blockbuster franchise.
It's a science fiction fantasy **which/that** has become a blockbuster franchise.

GRAMMAR PLUS see page 144

A Combine the sentences using relative pronouns. Then compare with a partner.
1. Jennifer Hudson is a singer. She's acted in several films.
2. *The Phantom of the Opera* is based on a French novel. It was published in 1911.
3. *Spiderman* and *Transformers* are successful franchises. They were adapted from comic books.
4. Michael Keaton is a famous Hollywood actor. He began his career as a cameraman.
5. Dakota Fanning is an actress. She made her first movie when she was only seven years old.
6. Wii Fit is a video game. It helps people to get more exercise.
7. Stephenie Meyer is an American writer. She wrote the *Twilight* series.
8. Many Hollywood stars live in Beverly Hills. It's a small city near Los Angeles, California.

Jennifer Hudson

B PAIR WORK Complete these sentences. Then compare your information around the class.
1. Adele is a singer and songwriter . . .
2. *Fantastic Four* is a movie franchise . . .
3. *The Voice* is a reality show . . .
4. Scarlett Johansson is an actress . . .

10 INTERCHANGE 13 It was hilarious!

How do you like movies and TV shows? Go to Interchange 13 on page 127.

That's entertainment!

11 SPEAKING Pilot episode

A PAIR WORK A TV studio is looking for ideas for a new TV show. Brainstorm possible ideas and agree on an idea. Make brief notes.

What kind of TV show is it?
What's it about?
Who are the main characters?
Who is this show for?

B CLASS ACTIVITY Tell the class about your TV show.

"Our TV show is a comedy. It's about two very lazy friends who discover a time machine and travel to the time of the dinosaurs. Then . . ."

12 LISTENING At the movies

A Listen to two critics, Nicole and Anthony, talk about a new movie. Check (✓) the features of the movie that they discuss. (There are two extra features.)

	Nicole's opinion	Anthony's opinion
☐ acting		
☐ story		
☐ writing		
☐ music		
☐ love story		
☐ special effects		

B Listen again. Write Nicole and Anthony's opinions of each feature.

13 WRITING A movie review

A PAIR WORK Choose a movie you both have seen and discuss it. Then write a review of it.

What was the movie about?
What did you like about it?
What didn't you like about it?
How was the acting?
How would you rate it?

B CLASS ACTIVITY Read your review to the class. Who else has seen the movie? Do they agree with your review?

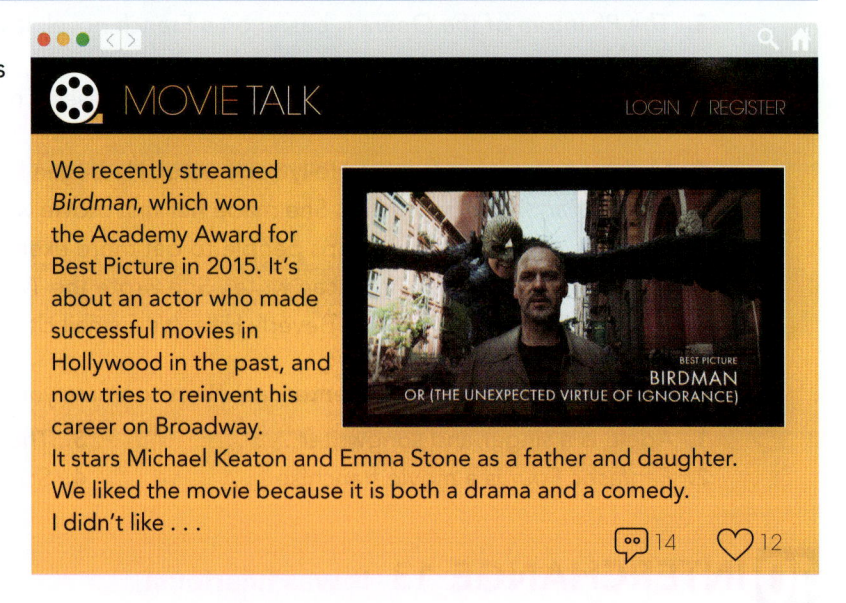

MOVIE TALK LOGIN / REGISTER

We recently streamed *Birdman*, which won the Academy Award for Best Picture in 2015. It's about an actor who made successful movies in Hollywood in the past, and now tries to reinvent his career on Broadway. It stars Michael Keaton and Emma Stone as a father and daughter. We liked the movie because it is both a drama and a comedy. I didn't like . . .

💬 14   ♥ 12

14 READING

A Scan the article. Which movies are mentioned? When were they released?

THE REAL ART OF ACTING

1 Acting can bring fame, money, and success. But it's not always easy. Good acting is not only about learning lines and dressing up. It's also about convincing the audience that you really are somebody else. _[a]_ To achieve this, good actors sometimes put themselves through unpleasant experiences.

2 Actors often have to lose or gain a lot of weight in order to play a part. In *The Machinist* (2005), Christian Bale plays an extremely thin factory worker who suffers from insomnia. _[b]_ Four months before he began filming, Bale started a crazy diet. He only ate an apple and a can of tuna a day and lost 63 pounds. Although he wanted to lose another 20 pounds, the producers persuaded him to stop because they were worried about his health. When filming ended, he had just six months to gain the incredible 100 pounds he needed to play Bruce Wayne in *Batman Begins*. _[c]_

3 Physical training can also be a challenge. Steven Spielberg wanted to show the real horror of war in *Saving Private Ryan* (1998) and he wanted his actors to feel like real soldiers. So he sent a group of them, including Tom Hanks, to a 10-day military boot camp. _[d]_ They ran miles every day, slept outside in the freezing cold, and were given little food. In the end, all of them were physically and mentally exhausted. Natalie Portman also had to make a great physical effort when she got the role of a ballerina in *Black Swan* (2010). Before filming, she spent a whole year training for eight hours a day, six days a week in order to learn to dance. Once filming began, things didn't get easier either. Portman dislocated a rib while dancing. Nevertheless, she bravely continued filming during the six weeks it took her to recover.

4 Sometimes "becoming" a character can mean saying goodbye to the real world and everybody in it completely. Actor Heath Ledger locked himself in a hotel room for six weeks when he was preparing to play the role of Joker in *The Dark Knight* (2008). He slept only two hours a day and he spent the rest of the time practicing how to walk, talk, and move like his character. _[e]_ It seems he was successful in the end, as audiences and critics loved his work, and he won an Oscar for the part.

B Read the article. Where do these sentences belong? Write a–e.

1. The actors' lives became very hard. ____
2. Not sleeping is making him sick. ____
3. And he didn't speak to anybody at all. ____
4. The character has to be believable. ____
5. So he ate lots of pizza and ice cream. ____

C Find words in the text to match these definitions.

1. The words that actors say in a movie (paragraph 1) _____
2. People who control how a movie is made (paragraph 2) _____
3. A bone in a person's chest (paragraph 3) _____
4. The people who write reviews of movies or books (paragraph 4) _____

D Which of these unpleasant experiences is the worst? Do you think it's necessary for an actor to do this kind of thing for a part?

That's entertainment!

14 Now I get it!

▶ Discuss the meaning of gestures and body language
▶ Discuss rules and recognize common signs

1 SNAPSHOT

POPULAR EMOJIS

- I am not amused.
- I'm laughing so hard, I'm crying!
- I'm bored.
- Great job!
- That's amazing!
- I'm so embarrassed.
- I love it!
- That's awful!
- Just kidding!
- My heart is breaking.

Do you use these emojis? In what situations do you use them?
What other expressions can you use emojis to convey?
What is the weirdest emoji you've ever seen? the funniest? the hardest to understand?

2 WORD POWER Body language

A What is this woman doing in each picture? Match each description with a picture. Then compare with a partner.

1. She's scratching her head. _____
2. She's biting her nails. _____
3. She's rolling her eyes. _____
4. She's tapping her foot. _____
5. She's pulling her hair out. _____
6. She's wrinkling her nose. _____

B **GROUP WORK** Use the pictures in part A and these adjectives to describe how the woman is feeling.

| annoyed | confused | embarrassed | frustrated | irritated |
| bored | disgusted | exhausted | impatient | nervous |

"In the first picture, she's tapping her foot. She looks impatient."

3 CONVERSATION It's pretty confusing.

A Listen and practice.

Eva: How was dinner with the new Bulgarian student last night? What's her name – Elena?

Brian: Yeah, Elena. It was nice. We always have a good time, but I still don't understand her very well. You see, when we offer her something to eat or drink, she nods her head up and down. But, at the same time she says no.

Eva: It might mean she wants to accept it, but she thinks it's not polite. In some countries, you have to refuse any offer first. Then the host insists, and you accept it.

Brian: I don't know . . . It's pretty confusing.

Eva: It could mean she doesn't want anything, but she thinks it's rude to say no.

Jack: Actually, in some countries, when people move their heads up and down, it means "no."

Brian: Really? Now I get it!

B Now listen to Elena talk to her friend. What does she find unusual about the way people in North America communicate?

4 GRAMMAR FOCUS

Modals and adverbs

Modals
It **might/may** mean she wants to accept it.
It **could** mean she doesn't want anything.
That **must** mean "no."

Adverbs
Maybe/Perhaps it means she wants to accept it.
It **probably** means she doesn't want anything.
That **definitely** means "no."

GRAMMAR PLUS see page 145

PAIR WORK What do these gestures mean? Take turns making statements about each gesture. Use the meanings in the box or your own ideas.

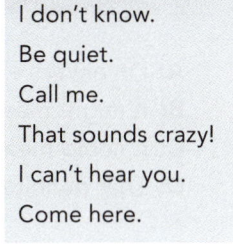

possible meanings
I don't know.
Be quiet.
Call me.
That sounds crazy!
I can't hear you.
Come here.

A: What do you think the first gesture means?
B: It probably means . . . , OR It might mean . . .

Now I get it! 93

5 PRONUNCIATION Pitch

A Listen and practice. Notice how pitch is used to express certainty or doubt.

	Certain	Uncertain
A: Do you think her gesture means "no"?	B: Definitely.	B: Probably.
A: Do you understand what her gesture means?	B: Absolutely.	B: Maybe.

B **PAIR WORK** Take turns asking yes/no questions. Respond by using *absolutely*, *definitely*, *maybe*, *probably*, and your own information. Pay attention to pitch.

6 SPEAKING What's the matter with me?

A **GROUP WORK** Imagine you have one of these problems. What could explain it?

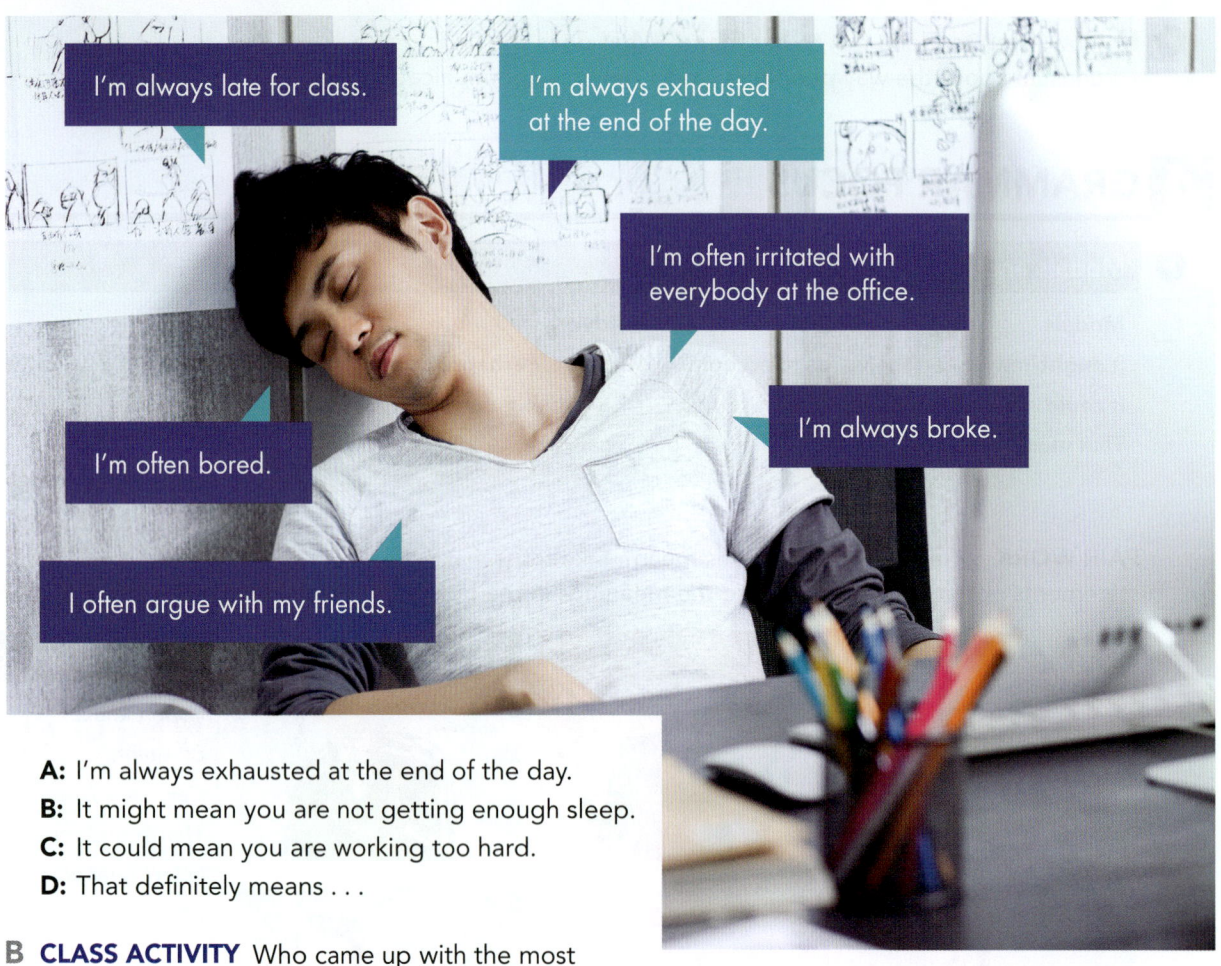

- I'm always late for class.
- I'm always exhausted at the end of the day.
- I'm often irritated with everybody at the office.
- I'm always broke.
- I'm often bored.
- I often argue with my friends.

A: I'm always exhausted at the end of the day.
B: It might mean you are not getting enough sleep.
C: It could mean you are working too hard.
D: That definitely means . . .

B **CLASS ACTIVITY** Who came up with the most interesting explanation in your group? the most unexpected?

7 INTERCHANGE 14 Casual observers

Interpret people's body language. Go to Interchange 14 on page 128.

8 PERSPECTIVES Rules and regulations

A What do you think these signs mean? Listen and match each sign with the correct meaning.

1. ___ 2. ___ 3. ___ 4. ___
5. ___ 6. ___ 7. ___ 8. ___

a. You can swim here.
b. You aren't allowed to take photos here.
c. You have to fasten your seat belts.
d. You've got to take off your shoes to enter.
e. You are allowed to park here.
f. You can't turn left.
g. Pets aren't allowed in this area.
h. You have to turn off electronic devices in this area.

B **PAIR WORK** Where might you see the signs in part A? Give two suggestions for each one.

"You might see this one by a lake . . ."

9 GRAMMAR FOCUS

Permission, obligation, and prohibition

Permission	Obligation	Prohibition
You **can** swim here.	You **have to** fasten your seat belt.	You **can't** turn left.
You**'re allowed to** park here.	You**'ve got to** take off your shoes.	Pets **aren't allowed** in this area.

GRAMMAR PLUS see page 145

A **PAIR WORK** Use the language in the grammar box to talk about these signs.

A: This first sign means you've got to use the stairs in case of a fire.
B: Yes, I think you're right. And the second one means you aren't allowed to . . .

B **CLASS ACTIVITY** What are some of the rules in your office or school?

A: In my office, we can't eat at our desks.
B: We can't either, but we're allowed to have water.
C: We're allowed to eat at our desks, but we have to clean up afterward.

Now I get it!

10 DISCUSSION Play by the rules.

A PAIR WORK How many rules can you think of for each of these places?

at the gym   at a public swimming pool   on an airplane
in a museum   in a movie theater   at work

"At the gym, you have to wear sneakers or other athletic shoes. You're not allowed to wear regular shoes."

B GROUP WORK Share your ideas. Why do you think these rules exist? Have you ever broken any of them? What happened?

11 LISTENING Road signs

A Listen to four conversations about driving. Number the situations they are discussing in the correct order from 1 to 4.

____ Cars can't be in the bus and taxi lane.
____ Drivers must drive within the speed limit.
____ Drivers have to turn on car headlights on mountain roads.
____ Cars are allowed to park in this area after 6:00 P.M.

B Listen again. How did they find out about the traffic situation? Write what happened.

1. _____
2. _____
3. _____
4. _____

C PAIR WORK How do you move around your city? Give two examples of traffic laws you must obey.

12 WRITING Golden rules

A GROUP WORK Discuss the rules that currently exist at your school. How many can you think of? Are they all good rules?

B GROUP WORK Think of four new rules that you feel would be a good idea. Work together to write brief explanations of why each is necessary.

1. You aren't allowed to use your first language. If you need to use it, you need to ask your teacher for permission.
2. You have to pay a small fine if you hand in your homework late.
3. You can be late, but you have to come in quietly so you don't disturb the lesson.

C CLASS ACTIVITY Share your lists. Vote on the best new rules.

13 READING

A Skim the article. Match the pictures 1, 2, and 3 to the paragraphs.

UNDERSTANDING IDIOMS

Idioms can be a problem for language learners. They often seem to make absolutely no sense at all. For example, imagine your English friend Sam tells you his math exam was "a piece of cake." Do you imagine him at school, sitting in front of a sweet dessert with nothing but a pen to eat it with? In fact, he's saying that the exam was really easy. It's important to learn useful English idioms and knowing their origins helps us to remember them. Here are stories of three English idioms.

____ A If you ask a friend to hang out, you might hear, "Sorry, I can't tonight. I'm feeling a little under the weather." It may sound like rain is coming, but really, it means that your friend feels sick. This expression came from sailors, who often got seasick when bad weather tossed the ship from side to side. The sailors went down to the bottom part of the ship, away from the storm and where the ship's rocking was gentler.

____ B If you have a difficult roommate, you might say, "My roommate has loud parties every night, but last night was the last straw. They played music till 5 A.M.! I'm moving out." A "last straw" is a final problem that makes someone take action. This expression is a short form of the phrase "the straw that broke the camel's back." The idea is that even though a single piece of straw is very light, many pieces added together will be too heavy for the camel to carry.

____ C Have you ever asked someone if they know something, and they reply, "That rings a bell"? They're not hearing music! They mean that what you're saying sounds familiar, and they think they've heard it before. This idiom comes from the fact that bells are used to remind people of many things. Traditionally, bells would toll for an important event, like a wedding. School bells tell you that class is starting, and even the alarm chime on your phone reminds you that it's time to get up.

B Read the article and correct the false statements below.

1. You can guess the meaning of an idiom if you understand each word.
   _____

2. In the past, people knew about important events when they heard shouting.
   _____

3. A camel falls down if it has to carry too much water.
   _____

4. Sailors used to feel sicker when they went to the bottom of the ship.
   _____

C Complete the sentences with the correct form of one of the idioms.

1. Julie has a bad cold at the moment, and she's _____.
2. I don't remember his face, but his name _____.
3. When the neighbors' noisy kids broke my window with their ball, it _____.

D What idioms are commonly used in your country? Where do you think they come from?

Now I get it! 97

Units 13–14 Progress check

SELF-ASSESSMENT

How well can you do these things? Check (✓) the boxes.

I can . . .	Very well	OK	A little
Ask about and express opinions and emotions (Ex. 1, 4, 5)	☐	☐	☐
Discuss movies (Ex. 2)	☐	☐	☐
Understand descriptions of rules and laws (Ex. 3)	☐	☐	☐
Speculate about things when I'm not sure and recognize emotions (Ex. 4)	☐	☐	☐
Describe rules and laws: permission, obligation, and prohibition (Ex. 5)	☐	☐	☐

1 SURVEY Personal preferences

A Complete the first column of the survey with your opinions.

	Me	My classmate
A fascinating book		
A confusing movie		
A boring TV show		
A shocking news story		
An interesting celebrity		
A singer you are amazed by		
A song you are annoyed by		

B **CLASS ACTIVITY** Go around the class and find someone who has the same opinions. Write a classmate's name only once.

"I thought *I am Malala* was a fascinating book. What about you?"

2 ROLE PLAY Movie night

Student A: Invite Student B to a movie. Suggest two movie options.
Then answer your partner's questions.
Start like this: *Do you want to see a movie?*

Student B: Student A invites you to a movie.
Find out more about the movie.
Then accept or refuse the invitation.

Change roles and try the role play again.

3 LISTENING Unusual laws around the world

A Listen to two people discuss an article about laws in different places. Match the topic to the place. (There are two extra topics.)

a. smiling	b. chewing gum	c. stealing
d. hospitals	e. pigeons	f. carrying money

1. Singapore ____   2. Kenya ____   3. San Francisco ____   4. Milan ____

B Listen again. Complete the sentences to describe each law.

1. In Singapore, you _____.
2. In Kenya, you _____.
3. In San Francisco, you _____.
4. In Milan, you _____.

C PAIR WORK Which law seems the strangest to you? the most logical? Why?

4 GAME Miming

A Think of two emotions or ideas you can communicate with gestures. Write them on separate cards.

B GROUP WORK Shuffle your cards together. Then take turns picking cards and acting out the meanings with gestures. The student who guesses correctly goes next.

A: That probably means you're disgusted.
B: No.
C: It could mean you're surprised.
B: You're getting closer . . .

I'm confused. I don't understand what you really want.

5 DISCUSSION What's the law?

GROUP WORK Read these laws from the United States. What do you think about them? Are they the same or different in your country?

- You aren't allowed to keep certain wild animals as pets.
- You're allowed to vote when you turn 18.
- In some states, you can get married when you're 16.
- You have to wear a seat belt in the back seat of a car in most states.
- Young men don't have to serve in the military.
- In some states, you can't drive faster than 65 miles per hour (about 100 kph).
- In most states, children have to attend school until they are 16 or 18.

A: In the U.S.A., you aren't allowed to keep certain wild animals as pets.
B: It's the same for us. You've got to have a special permit to keep a wild animal.
C: I've heard that in some countries, you can keep lions and tigers as pets.

WHAT'S NEXT?

Look at your Self-assessment again. Do you need to review anything?

15 I wouldn't have done that.

▸ Discuss imaginary situations
▸ Discuss difficult situations

1 SNAPSHOT

NEWS 4 YOU | NEW TODAY | MOST POPULAR | TRENDING | LOGIN | SIGN UP

FLORIDA MOM "CAUGHT" BEING HONEST
Nancy Bloom was caught on the security camera entering a convenience store while the owner was out to lunch. The door was unlocked, so Nancy walked in with her son, picked up some ice cream, and left the money on the counter.

MOST SHARED THIS WEEK

HONESTY IS ITS OWN REWARD
After driving for 20 miles to return a wallet lost in a park, Kate Moore gets only a half-hearted, "Oh. Thanks."

HOMELESS MAN FINDS $40,000 AND TURNS IT IN
When Tom Heart found a backpack full of cash, he didn't think twice. He took it straight to the police. After reading Tom's story, a stranger started a fundraising campaign for Tom that has already raised over $60,000.

Have you heard any stories like these recently?
Have you ever found anything valuable? What did you do?
Do you think that people who return lost things should get a reward?

2 CONVERSATION What would you do?

A Listen and practice.

Joon: Look at this. A homeless guy found a backpack with $40,000 inside!
Mia: And what did he do?
Joon: He took it to the police. He gave it all back, every single penny.
Mia: You're kidding! If I found $40,000, I wouldn't return it. I'd keep it.
Joon: Really? What would you do with it?
Mia: Well, I'd spend it. I could buy a new car or take a nice long vacation.
Joon: The real owner might find out about it, though, and then you could go to jail.
Mia: Hmm. You've got a point there.

B Listen to the rest of the conversation. What would Joon do if he found $40,000?

3 GRAMMAR FOCUS

Unreal conditional sentences with *if* clauses

Imaginary situation (simple past)	Possible consequence (*would*, *could*, or *might* + verb)
If I **found** $40,000,	I **would keep** it. I **wouldn't return** it. I **could buy** a new car. I **might go** to the police.

What **would** you **do if** you **found** $40,000?

GRAMMAR PLUS see page 146

A Complete these conversations. Then compare with a partner.

1. **A:** What _____ you _____ (do) if you lost your sister's favorite sweater?
   B: Of course I _____ (buy) her a new one.
2. **A:** If you _____ (have) three months to travel, where _____ you _____ (go)?
   B: Oh, that's easy! I _____ (fly) to Europe. I've always wanted to go there.
3. **A:** If your doctor _____ (tell) you to get more exercise, which activity _____ you _____ (choose)?
   B: I'm not sure, but I think I _____ (go) jogging two or three times a week.
4. **A:** _____ you _____ (break) into your house if you _____ (lock) yourself out?
   B: No way! If I _____ (not have) another key, I _____ (ask) a neighbor for help.
5. **A:** If your friend _____ (want) to marry someone you didn't like, _____ you _____ (say) something?
   B: No, I _____ (not say) anything. I _____ (mind) my own business.
6. **A:** What _____ you _____ (do) if you _____ (see) your favorite movie star on the street?
   B: I _____ (not be) shy! I _____ (ask) to take a photo with them.

B **PAIR WORK** Take turns asking the questions in part A. Answer with your own information.

4 LISTENING Tough situations

A Listen to three people talk about predicaments. Check which predicament they are talking about.

1. ☐ Chris has relationship problems.   ☐ Chris is addicted to the Internet.
2. ☐ Kari spent all her money in Europe.   ☐ Kari lost all her money in Europe.
3. ☐ Zoey saw her classmates cheating.   ☐ Zoey doesn't understand her math class.

B Listen again. Write the two suggestions given for each predicament.

1. a. _____ b. _____
2. a. _____ b. _____
3. a. _____ b. _____

C **GROUP WORK** Which suggestions do you agree with? Why?

I wouldn't have done that.

5 INTERCHANGE 15 Tough choices

What would you do in some difficult situations? Go to Interchange 15 on page 130.

6 WORD POWER Opposites

A Find nine pairs of opposites in this list. Complete the chart. Then compare with a partner.

accept	borrow	dislike	find	lose	remember
admit	deny	divorce	forget	marry	save
agree	disagree	enjoy	lend	refuse	spend

accept	≠	refuse		≠			≠
	≠			≠			≠
	≠			≠			≠

B PAIR WORK Choose four pairs of opposites. Write sentences using each pair.

> I can't remember my dreams. As soon as I wake up, I forget them.

7 PERSPECTIVES That was a big mistake.

A Listen to people talk about recent predicaments. Then check (✓) the best suggestion for each one.

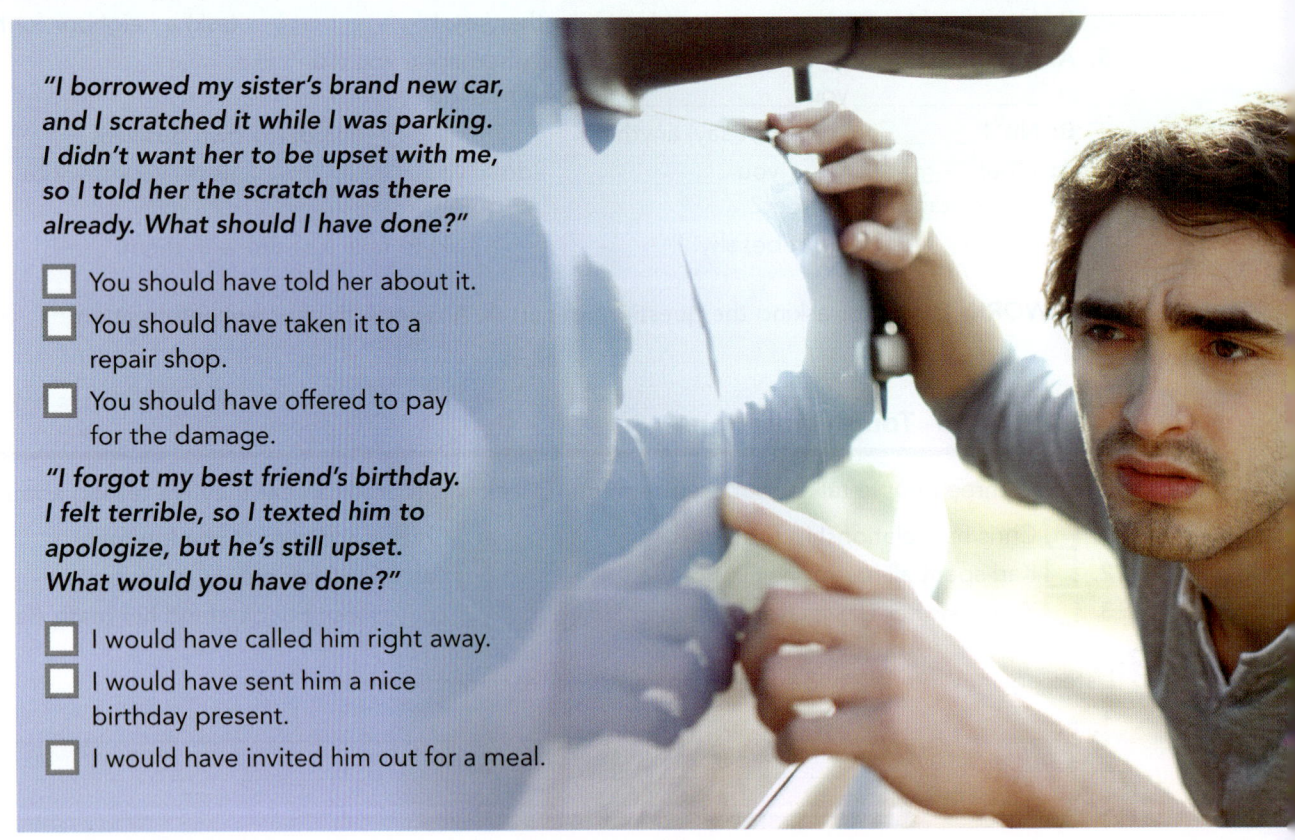

"I borrowed my sister's brand new car, and I scratched it while I was parking. I didn't want her to be upset with me, so I told her the scratch was there already. What should I have done?"

☐ You should have told her about it.
☐ You should have taken it to a repair shop.
☐ You should have offered to pay for the damage.

"I forgot my best friend's birthday. I felt terrible, so I texted him to apologize, but he's still upset. What would you have done?"

☐ I would have called him right away.
☐ I would have sent him a nice birthday present.
☐ I would have invited him out for a meal.

B PAIR WORK Compare with a partner. Do you agree with each other?

8 GRAMMAR FOCUS

Past modals

Use **would have** or **should have** + past participle to give opinions or suggestions about actions in the past.

What **should I have done**?	You **should have told** her about it.
	You **shouldn't have lied** to your sister.
What **would you have done**?	I **would have called** him.
	I **wouldn't have texted** him.

GRAMMAR PLUS see page 146

A Complete these conversations. Then practice with a partner.

1. **A:** I was in a meeting at work when my girlfriend texted me saying she needed to see me right away. What should I have _____ (do)?
   B: You should have _____ (send) her a message and _____ (tell) her you'd call back later.

2. **A:** The cashier gave me too much change. What should I have _____ (do)?
   B: You should have _____ (say) something. You shouldn't have _____ (take) the money.

3. **A:** I ignored an email from someone I don't like. What would you have _____ (do)?
   B: I would have _____ (reply) to the person. It just takes a minute!

4. **A:** We left all our trash at the campsite. What would you have _____ (do)?
   B: I would have _____ (take) it with me and _____ (throw) it away later.

B Read the situations below. What would have been the best thing to do? Choose suggestions. Then compare with a partner.

Situations

1. The teacher borrowed my favorite book and spilled coffee all over it. _____
2. I saw a classmate cheating on an exam, so I wrote her an email about it. _____
3. A friend of mine always has messy hair, so I gave him a comb for his birthday. _____
4. I hit someone's car when I was leaving a parking lot. Luckily, no one saw me. _____
5. My aunt gave me a wool sweater. I can't wear wool, so I gave it back. _____

Suggestions

a. You should have spoken to him about it.
b. I would have spoken to the teacher about it.
c. I would have waited for the owner to return.
d. I wouldn't have said anything.
e. You should have warned her not to do it again.
f. You should have left a note for the owner.
g. I would have told her that I prefer something else.
h. You should have exchanged it for something else.

C GROUP WORK Make another suggestion for each situation in part B.

9 PRONUNCIATION Reduction of *have*

A Listen and practice. Notice how **have** is reduced in these sentences.

/əv/
What would you have done?

/əv/
I would have told the truth.

B PAIR WORK Practice the conversations in Exercise 8, part A, again. Use the reduced form of **have**.

I wouldn't have done that. **103**

10 LISTENING Problem solved!

A Listen to an advice podcast. Complete the chart.

	Problem	What the person did
Ronnie:		
Becca:		

B Listen again. According to Dr. Jones, what should each person have done?

Ronnie: _____

Becca: _____

C PAIR WORK What would you have done in each situation?

11 SPEAKING An awful trip

A PAIR WORK Imagine a friend has been on a really awful trip and everything went wrong. What should your friend have done? What shouldn't he or she have done?

Your friend spent hours in the sun and got a sunburn.
Your friend drank tap water and got sick.
Your friend stayed at a very bad hotel.
Your friend's wallet was stolen.
Your friend overslept and missed the flight back.

A: She shouldn't have spent so many hours in the sun.
B: She should have used sunscreen.

B GROUP WORK Have you ever had any bad experiences on a trip? What happened?

12 WRITING Advice needed

Write a post to a community blog about a real or imaginary problem.
Put your drafts on the wall and choose one to write a reply to.

WHAT WENT WRONG?
submitted by dmartin 10 hours ago

I lent my girlfriend $10,000 to help her pay for her college tuition. That was about a year ago, and at the time, she said she would pay me back as soon as she found a job. She never even looked for a job. Last week, I asked her for my money back, and she accused me of being selfish, unsympathetic, and insensitive. She broke up with me, and now she won't even talk to me anymore. What did I do wrong? What should I have done? What should I do now? Does anyone have any suggestions?

248 comments

13 READING

A Skim the three posts. What do Jack, Maya, and Andrés ask for advice about?

TOPTIPS.COM

1 JACK – LONDON ♡12

I am overweight, and I'd really like to slim down. I've tried all kinds of diets, but none of them seem to work. And there's so much advice on the Internet – I don't know what to believe any more. What would you recommend?

I had the same problem until I tried a high protein/no carbohydrate diet. It was very strict – in the first couple of weeks you have to eat less than 40 grams of carbohydrates a day, so no bread, pasta, or potatoes! But I lost nine pounds in just 13 days, so for me it was worth it. I had a lot of meat and eggs and some butter, too, which was great! I'd give it a shot if I were you. (Sarah, Edinburgh)

2 MAYA – SAN FRANCISCO ♡22

I'm traveling to Rio de Janeiro next month, and I'd like to see as much of the city as possible. The problem is that I'm only going to be there for a couple of days, and I'm not sure how to fit everything in. Should I book an organized tour?

I was in Rio a couple of months ago. I travel a lot and like to be independent, so I chose to find my own way around the city. What a mistake! Rio's so big that I kept getting lost! And in the end, I didn't get to see the beach of Ipanema or the cathedral. It would have been nice to have somebody to talk to also. I really should have gone on a guided tour. (Dag, Oslo)

3 ANDRÉS – BOGOTÁ ♡11

I've just finished my degree, and I'm on the fence about what to do next. Here in Bogotá, there aren't many job possibilities right now. Should I go back to college to get a Master's? Or go stay with my cousin in New York and try to get a job there? (My English is not very good, by the way – a friend wrote this!)

Stay where you are! I moved to the United States from Poland and got a job as a server, but it's long hours and not much money. I haven't really made many friends, and I miss home. I should have stayed there and continued with my studies. (Marta, Krakow)

B Read the posts. Who would say these sentences? Write names from the posts.

1. Should I go abroad or stay where I am? _____
2. It worked for me, so why don't you try it? _____
3. I would have been happier if I hadn't moved. _____
4. How can I choose the right eating plan? _____
5. If I went there again, I'd definitely join a group. _____
6. I don't have much time, so I need to be organized. _____

C Find words or expressions in the posts to match these definitions.

1. Be an important or useful thing to do (post 1) _____
2. Find enough time for something (post 2) _____
3. To be unable to make a decision (post 3) _____

D Do you agree with the advice given above? What advice would you give?

I wouldn't have done that.

16 Making excuses

▸ Give reasons and explanations
▸ Discuss statements other people made

1 SNAPSHOT

Good Excuses, Poor Excuses

Not doing homework
- I was sure the assignment was due tomorrow.
- I emailed it to you, but it bounced back.

Arriving late to class
- My father didn't wake me up.
- My bike tire was flat because a dog bit it.

Missing work
- My cat was sick, and I had to take care of her.
- It was my birthday, and I always donate blood on that day.

Arriving late to work
- I worked on the new project until four in the morning, and then I overslept.
- My wife thinks it's funny to hide my car keys in the morning.

Arriving late for a date
- I was taking a telephone survey and lost track of the time.
- A horse running on the highway was holding up traffic.

Which are good excuses? Which are poor ones?
What excuse do you usually use for these situations?
What excuses can you make for missing a date or party?

2 PERSPECTIVES At your request

A Who do you think made these requests? Listen and match.

1. She said to arrive on time for the meeting. ____
2. She asked me to pick up some food on the way home. ____
3. He said not to miss practice again. ____
4. She told me to hand in my homework before Friday. ____
5. She said to drink at least six glasses of water a day. ____
6. He asked me not to tell Mom about his new girlfriend. ____
7. He told me not to leave my bike in the apartment hallway. ____

a. my teacher
b. my boss
c. my brother
d. my doctor
e. my neighbor
f. my roommate
g. my coach

B PAIR WORK Can you think of another request each person might make?

A: Our teacher sometimes says, "Open your books."
B: A teacher could also say, "Repeat after me."

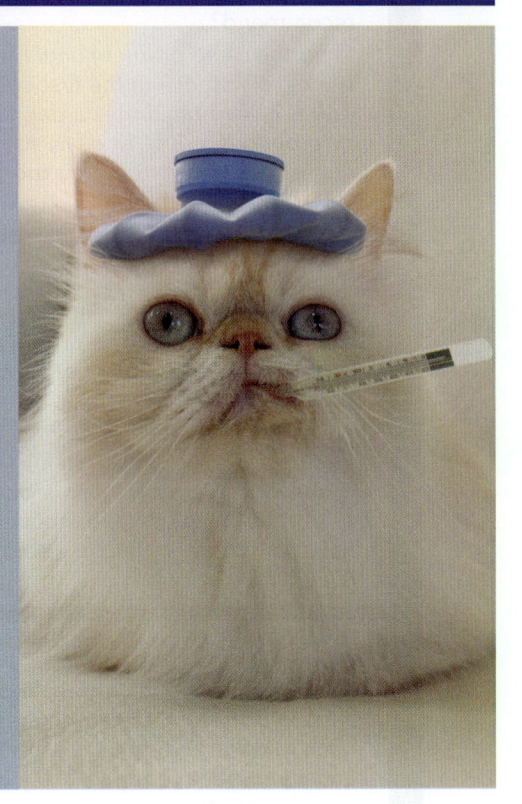

3 GRAMMAR FOCUS

▶ Reported speech: requests

Original request	Reported request
Arrive on time for the meeting.	She **said to arrive** on time for the meeting.
	She **told me to arrive** on time for the meeting.
Don't leave your bike in the apartment hallway.	He **said not to leave** my bike in the hallway.
	He **told me not to leave** my bike in the hallway.
Can you pick up some food on the way home?	She **asked me to pick up** some food.

GRAMMAR PLUS see page 147

A Victor is organizing a surprise birthday party for his teacher. Look at what he told his classmates. Write each request using *say*, *tell*, or *ask*. Then compare with a partner.

1. Meet at my apartment at 7:30.   _He told them to meet at his apartment at 7:30._
2. Don't arrive late.   _____
3. Can you bring some ice cream?   _____
4. Can you help me make the sandwiches?   _____
5. Can you bring a small gift for her?   _____
6. Don't spend more than $10 on the gift.   _____
7. Keep the party a secret.   _____
8. Don't say anything to the other teachers.   _____

B GROUP WORK Imagine you're planning a class party. Write four requests. Then take turns reading your requests and changing them into reported requests.

Edu: Bring something to eat to the party!
Eva: Edu told us to bring something to eat.

Aki: Can you help me clean up after the party?
Jim: Aki asked us to help her clean up.

4 SPEAKING That's asking too much!

A Think of requests that people have made recently. Write two things people asked you to do and two things people asked you *not* to do.

Person	Request
My boss	shave off my beard

B GROUP WORK Talk about the requests that each of you listed in part A. Did you do what people requested? Did you give an excuse? What was it?

Making excuses

5 WORD POWER Verb-noun collocations

A Find three more nouns that are usually paired with each verb. The same noun can be paired with more than one verb. Then compare with a partner.

an apology	an invitation	a request
a complaint	a joke	a solution
an excuse	a lie	a story
an explanation	an offer	a suggestion
an idea	a reason	the truth

make	a request			
give	an excuse			
tell	a joke			
accept	an apology			
refuse	an invitation			

B **PAIR WORK** How do you deal with the things in part A? Tell a partner.

A: What do you do when a close friend makes a difficult request?
B: I give a good explanation, and I offer to help in another way. What about you?

6 CONVERSATION Are you doing anything on Sunday?

A Listen and practice.

Gabriel: Hi, Craig.

Craig: Oh, hi, Gabriel. How are things?

Gabriel: Just fine, thanks. Uh, are you doing anything on Sunday night?

Craig: Hmm. Sunday night? Let me think. Oh, yes. My brother just called, and he told me he had tickets to the basketball finals. I said I would go with him.

Gabriel: Oh, that's too bad! It's my birthday. I'm having dinner with Tina, and I thought I'd invite more people and make it a party.

Craig: Oh, I'm really sorry, but I won't be able to make it.

Gabriel: I'm sorry, too. But that's OK.

B **PAIR WORK** Act out the conversation in part A. Make up your own excuse for not accepting Gabriel's invitation.

7 LISTENING Making excuses

A Listen to Gabriel invite his friends to his birthday party on Saturday. What excuses do they give for not going? Write them below.

1. Grant: _____
2. Sayo: _____
3. Diego: _____
4. Carrie: _____

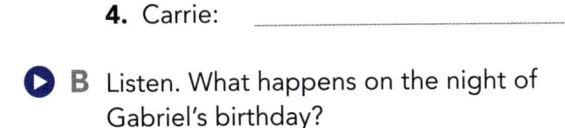

B Listen. What happens on the night of Gabriel's birthday?

C PAIR WORK What was the last party you went to? Describe it to your partner.

8 GRAMMAR FOCUS

Reported speech: statements

Direct statements	Reported statements
I'm not feeling well.	She said (that) she wasn't feeling well.
I have houseguests for the weekend.	she had houseguests for the weekend.
I made a tennis date with Kim.	she had made a tennis date with Kim.
I have planned an exciting trip.	she had planned an exciting trip.
We can't come tomorrow.	They told me (that) they couldn't come tomorrow.
We will be out of town.	they would be out of town.
We may go out with friends.	they might go out with friends.

GRAMMAR PLUS see page 147

A Isabella is having a party at her house on Saturday. Look at these excuses. Change them into reported speech. Then compare with a partner.

1. Mason: "I already have plans for Saturday."
2. Olivia: "My in-laws are coming over for dinner that night."
3. Ben and Ava: "We've been invited to a graduation party on Saturday."
4. Felipe: "I promised to help my sister with her homework."
5. Tae-yun: "I can't come because I broke my leg."
6. Osvaldo: "I'll be moving this weekend."
7. Lisa and Henry: "We have to pick someone up at the airport that evening."
8. Omar: "I may have to work the night shift on Saturday."

> Mason said he already had plans for Saturday. OR
> Mason told her he already had plans for Saturday.

B GROUP WORK Imagine you don't want to go to Isabella's party. Take turns making excuses and changing them into reported speech.

A: I'm sorry, I can't go. I'm going camping this weekend.
B: Lucky guy! He said he was going camping this weekend.

Making excuses

9 PRONUNCIATION Reduction of *had* and *would*

A Listen and practice. Notice how *had* and *would* are reduced in the following sentences.

She said she'**d made** the bed. (She said she **had made** the bed.)
She said she'**d make** the bed. (She said she **would make** the bed.)

B Listen to four sentences. Check (✓) the reduced form that you hear.

1. ☐ had   2. ☐ had   3. ☐ had   4. ☐ had
   ☐ would   ☐ would   ☐ would   ☐ would

10 WRITING About my classmates

A Interview your classmates and take notes. Use your notes to write a report describing what people told you. Use reported speech.

	Name	Response
What did you do last night?		
What movie have you seen recently?		
Where are you going after class?		
What are your plans for the weekend?		
What will you do on your next birthday?		

B GROUP WORK Read your report, but don't give names. Others guess the person.

"Someone said that he'd go to Paris on his next vacation."

11 SPEAKING You can make it.

A GROUP WORK What are some things you would like to do in the future? Think of three intentions.

A: I'm going to take an English course abroad.
B: That sounds fun. Have you decided where?

B CLASS ACTIVITY Report the best intentions you heard. Then give suggestions.

B: Noriko said she was going to take an English course abroad, but she hadn't decided where.
C: She could go to Australia. My brother attended a very good school there. He told me he studied incredibly hard!

12 INTERCHANGE 16 Just a bunch of excuses

Make some plans. Student A, go to Interchange 16A on page 129; Student B, go to Interchange 16B on page 131.

13 READING

A Scan the article. What are three common reasons for missing work?

A GOOD EXCUSE FOR A DAY OFF WORK

1 On average, U.S. employees take 4.9 sick days per year. Usually this does not cause any particular problems. But when employees take sick leave without a good reason, it can quickly become an issue. In fact, in one survey, 18 percent of employers said that they had fired an employee for taking days off without a good reason. The key is to understand what reasons are acceptable and what reasons are not. Generally, most excuses for sick days fall into one of three categories.

2 The most common reasons for not going to work are health-related. It would probably be OK to tell your boss that you ate something bad last night and that you have a stomachache. Of course you might not want to share the details of a health issue with your boss – after all, you do have the right to privacy. If you don't want to be too specific, you can just tell your boss that you have a small medical issue and need to take the day off.

3 Household accidents are the second category of reasons for not going in to work. You might call your boss to say you slipped in the shower and hurt your knee. This is a common accident and one that your boss will sympathize with. However, if you are going to be out of work for several days due to an injury, it's important to make arrangements with your employer. See if you can work from home, or at least make sure there is someone to cover your work.

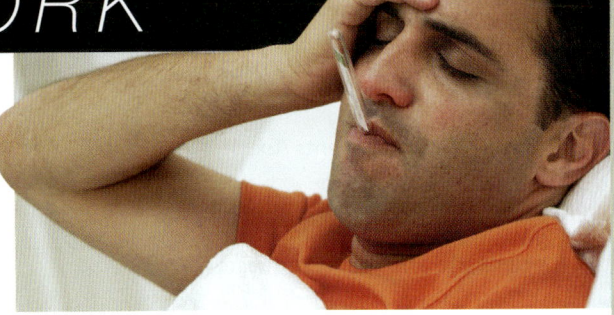

4 The third type of sick day use isn't really about illness, but it's about something else you can't control: transportation problems. The car might not start, there may be a terrible traffic jam, or there could be delays on the subway. Some employers may be sympathetic to absences due to transportation problems, but others may not. It's important to know your boss and to understand whether he or she will accept an excuse like this.

5 Regardless of the reason for the sick day, there are a few things you can do to make missing work more acceptable to your employer. Try to keep sick days to a minimum. When you do need to take a sick day, give your employer as much advance notice as possible. Finally, never take a sick day if there isn't anything wrong with you – the only good excuses are the ones that are true.

B Read the article. Then correct four mistakes in the summary of the article.

U.S. workers take just under a month in sick days a year. The least frequently used excuses are for health reasons. When employees take a sick day, it's important to explain the reason to their colleagues. It's OK to take a sick day, even if you feel fine, as long as you give an excuse.

C Find words in the text to match these definitions.

1. told someone to leave his or her job (paragraph 1) _____
2. an explanation given for something (paragraph 1) _____
3. someone's right to keep information about his or her personal life secret (paragraph 2) _____
4. understand or care about someone's problems (paragraph 3) _____
5. a warning that something is about to happen (paragraph 5) _____

D What other excuses do people make for not going to work or class? What's the silliest excuse you have ever heard?

Making excuses

Units 15–16 Progress check

SELF-ASSESSMENT

How well can you do these things? Check (✓) the boxes.

I can . . .	Very well	OK	A little
Discuss imaginary events (Ex. 1)	☐	☐	☐
Ask for and give advice and suggestions about past events (Ex. 2)	☐	☐	☐
Understand and report requests (Ex. 3)	☐	☐	☐
Discuss statements other people made (Ex. 4)	☐	☐	☐

1 DISCUSSION Interesting situations

A What would you do in these situations? Complete the statements.

If I forgot to do my homework, _____.
If I found a valuable piece of jewelry in the park, _____.
If a friend gave me a present I didn't like, _____.
If I wasn't invited to a party I wanted to attend, _____.
If someone took my clothes while I was swimming, _____.

B GROUP WORK Compare your responses. For each situation, choose one to tell the class.

A: What would you do if you forgot to do your homework?
B: I'd probably tell the teacher the truth. I'd ask her to let me hand it in next class.

2 SPEAKING Predicaments

A Make up two situations like the one below. Think about experiences you have had or heard about at work, home, or school.

"An old friend from high school visited me recently. We had a great time at first, but he became annoying. He made a big mess, and he left his things all over the place. After two weeks, I told him he had to leave because my sister was coming for the weekend."

B PAIR WORK Take turns sharing your situations. Ask for advice and suggestions.

A: What would you have done?
B: Well, I would have told him to pick up his clothes, and I would have asked him to clean up his mess.

3 LISTENING A small request

A Listen to the conversations. Check (✓) the person who is making the request.

1. ☐ child 2. ☐ neighbor 3. ☐ child 4. ☐ teacher 5. ☐ boss 6. ☐ neighbor
   ☐ parent   ☐ teacher   ☐ doctor   ☐ classmate   ☐ neighbor   ☐ teacher

B Listen again. Complete the requests.

1. Please _____ .
2. Can _____ ?
3. Don't _____ .
4. Can _____ ?
5. Please _____ .
6. Can _____ ?

C PAIR WORK Work with a partner. Imagine these requests were for you. Take turns reporting the requests to your partner.

"My dad told me to pick up my things."

4 GAME Who is lying?

A Think of situations when you expressed anger, gave an excuse, or made a complaint. Write a brief statement about each situation.

> I once complained about the bathroom in a hotel.

B CLASS ACTIVITY Play a game. Choose three students to be contestants.

Step 1: The contestants compare their statements and choose one. This statement should be true about only one student. The other two students should pretend they had the experience.

Step 2: The contestants stand in front of the class. Each contestant reads the same statement. The rest of the class must ask questions to find out who isn't telling the truth.

Contestant A, what hotel were you in?

Contestant B, what was wrong with the bathroom?

Contestant C, what did the manager do?

Step 3: Who isn't telling the truth? What did he or she say to make you think that?
"I don't think Contestant B is telling the truth. He said the bathroom was too small!"

WHAT'S NEXT?

Look at your Self-assessment again. Do you need to review anything?

This page is intentionally left blank

Interchange activities

INTERCHANGE 9 Cause and effect

A Read the questions on the cards. Check (✓) the box for your opinion.

1. If teens work part-time, they won't do well in school.
   - ☐ I agree.
   - ☐ I don't agree.
   - ☐ It depends.

2. If kids play violent video games, they will become violent themselves.
   - ☐ I agree.
   - ☐ I don't agree.
   - ☐ It depends.

3. If people decrease their screen time, they'll talk more with their families.
   - ☐ I agree.
   - ☐ I don't agree.
   - ☐ It depends.

4. If a woman gets married very early, she won't invest time in her career.
   - ☐ I agree.
   - ☐ I don't agree.
   - ☐ It depends.

5. If a woman works outside the home, her children won't be happy.
   - ☐ I agree.
   - ☐ I don't agree.
   - ☐ It depends.

6. If a child has brothers and sisters, he or she won't ever feel lonely.
   - ☐ I agree.
   - ☐ I don't agree.
   - ☐ It depends.

7. If you have too many online friends, you'll have fewer "real" friends.
   - ☐ I agree.
   - ☐ I don't agree.
   - ☐ It depends.

8. If there is a heavy fine for littering, our streets will be much cleaner.
   - ☐ I agree.
   - ☐ I don't agree.
   - ☐ It depends.

9. If people work only two days a week, their lives will improve.
   - ☐ I agree.
   - ☐ I don't agree.
   - ☐ It depends.

10. If teens have a lot of freedom, they will get in trouble more often.
    - ☐ I agree.
    - ☐ I don't agree.
    - ☐ It depends.

B **GROUP WORK** Compare your opinions. Be prepared to give reasons for your opinions.

A: I think if teens work part-time, they won't do well in school.
B: I don't really agree.
C: Why not?
B: If they work part-time, they'll become more responsible. That's a positive consequence.

INTERCHANGE 10 You're hired.

A PAIR WORK Look at the following job description. Write an ad for your ideal job.

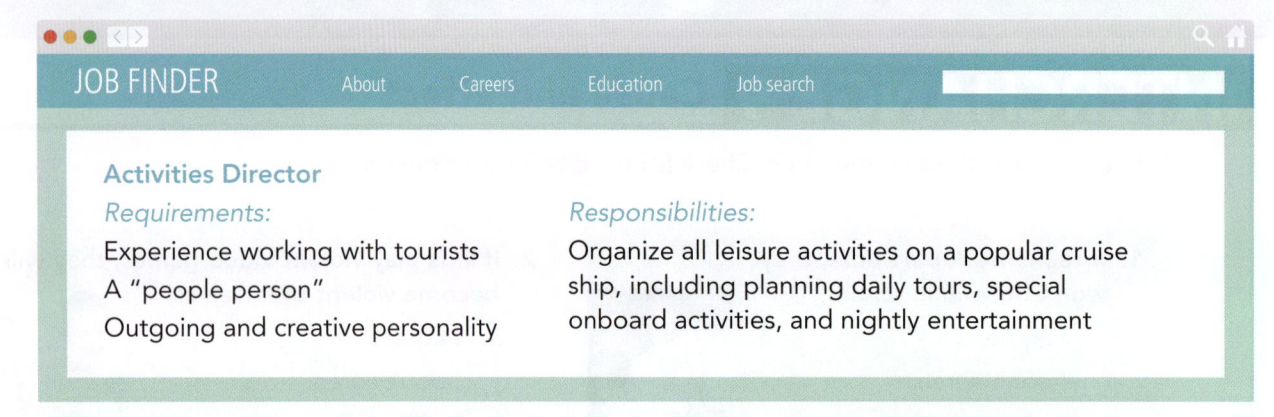

JOB FINDER   About   Careers   Education   Job search

Activities Director

Requirements:
Experience working with tourists
A "people person"
Outgoing and creative personality

Responsibilities:
Organize all leisure activities on a popular cruise ship, including planning daily tours, special onboard activities, and nightly entertainment

---

B PAIR WORK Take turns interviewing your classmates for the job you have created. Get as much information as you can to find the right person for the job.

useful questions

What kind of degree do you have?
What work experience do you have?
What hours can you work?
Do you mind . . . ?
Are you interested in . . . ?
Why should I hire you for the job?

C GROUP WORK Who would you hire for the job you posted? Why?

D CLASS ACTIVITY Compare the ideal jobs you created in part A. How are they similar? How are they different?

INTERCHANGE 11 True or false?

A List one movie, one TV show, one song, and one book.

B **GROUP WORK** Take turns making statements about each item. Does everyone agree with each statement?

   A: *Titanic* was filmed on a small lake in Mexico.
   B: Are you sure? Wasn't it filmed on the ocean?
   C: I'm pretty sure it was filmed in a plastic pool. I read it on the Internet.

C Now think of other famous creations and creators. Complete the chart. Make some of the items true and some false.

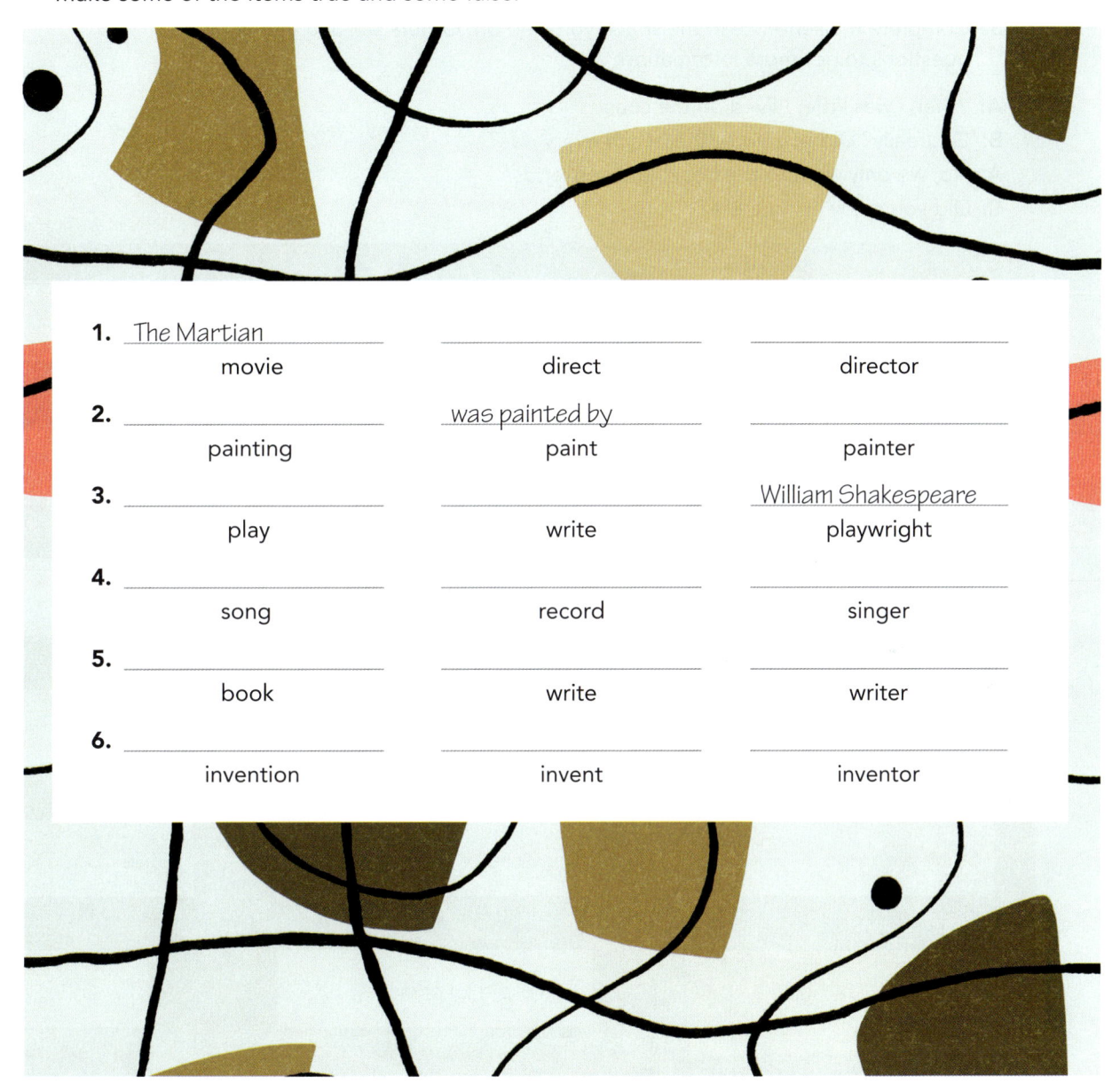

1. The Martian
   movie | direct | director
2. _____ | was painted by | _____
   painting | paint | painter
3. _____ | _____ | William Shakespeare
   play | write | playwright
4. _____ | _____ | _____
   song | record | singer
5. _____ | _____ | _____
   book | write | writer
6. _____ | _____ | _____
   invention | invent | inventor

D **GROUP WORK** Make a statement about each item to your group members. Ask them to decide which statements are true and which are false.

   A: The movie *The Martian* was directed by Steven Spielberg.
   B: I think that's true.
   C: No, that's false. It was directed by Ridley Scott. I'm sure of it.

INTERCHANGE 12 It's my life.

A GROUP WORK Play the board game. Follow these instructions.

1. Use small pieces of paper with your initials on them as markers.
2. Take turns tossing a coin:

   Move two spaces. **Heads**

   Move one space. **Tails**

3. Complete the sentence in the space you land on. Others ask two follow-up questions to get more information.

   A: When I was little, I lived on the coast.
   B: Oh, really? Did you go to the beach every day?
   A: No, we only went to the beach on weekends.
   C: Did you enjoy living there?

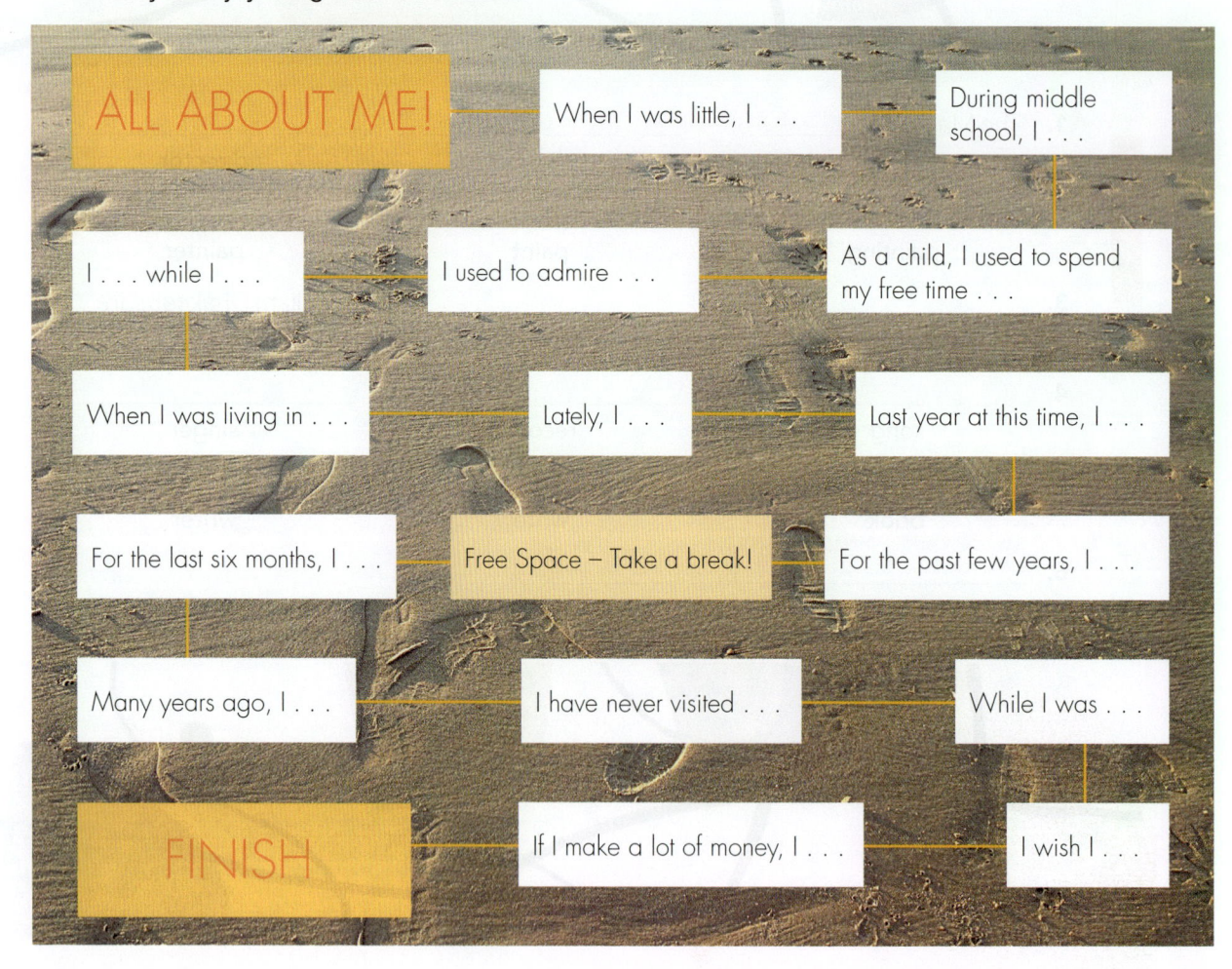

ALL ABOUT ME!

- When I was little, I . . .
- During middle school, I . . .
- I . . . while I . . .
- I used to admire . . .
- As a child, I used to spend my free time . . .
- When I was living in . . .
- Lately, I . . .
- Last year at this time, I . . .
- For the last six months, I . . .
- Free Space – Take a break!
- For the past few years, I . . .
- Many years ago, I . . .
- I have never visited . . .
- While I was . . .
- **FINISH**
- If I make a lot of money, I . . .
- I wish I . . .

B CLASS ACTIVITY Tell the class an interesting fact that you learned about someone in your group.

"For the last six months, Marcia has been taking dance classes."

INTERCHANGE 13 It was hilarious!

A Complete the questionnaire.

What is the name of a TV show or movie . . . ?

1. that made you laugh a lot

2. that made you feel sad

3. that you have seen more than once

4. which had great music

5. that was about a silly story

What is the name of a TV or movie star . . . ?

6. who is very talented

7. who is famous but not very talented

8. who does things to help society

9. who is an excellent comedian

10. that reminds you of someone you know

B **PAIR WORK** Compare your questionnaires. Ask follow-up questions of your own.

A: What's the name of a TV show or movie that made you laugh a lot?
B: *Grown Ups 2.*
A: Really? Why?
B: I thought the movie was hilarious.
A: Who was in it?
B: Adam Sandler. I always enjoy his movies.
A: Well, I liked his earlier movies better.

INTERCHANGE 14 Casual observers

A **PAIR WORK** Look at this scene of an airport. What do you think is happening in each of the situations? Look at people's body language for clues.

A: Why do you think the couple in situation 1 looks upset?
B: Well, they might be having a fight. They look . . .
A: Who do you think the woman in situation 6 is?
B: She must be famous. She might . . .

B **GROUP WORK** Compare your interpretations. Do you agree or disagree?

INTERCHANGE 16A Just a bunch of excuses

Student A

A **PAIR WORK** You and your partner want to get together. Ask and answer questions to find a day when you are both free. You also want to keep time open for other friends, so give excuses for those days. Write your partner's excuses on the calendar.

A: Do you want to meet on the 2nd?
B: I'm sorry. I'm going to an engagement party. Are you free on the 1st?
A: Well, I . . .

September

Sunday	Monday	Tuesday	Wednesday	Thursday	Friday	Saturday
					1 dinner with Pat	2
3	4 class	5	6	7 You want to keep this date free. Make an excuse.	8 party at Sam's	9
10	11 You want to keep this date free. Make an excuse.	12 bowling with Chris	13	14 movie with Haru	15	16
17 dinner with office friends	18 class	19	20	21 study for tomorrow's exam	22 You want to keep this date free. Make an excuse.	23
24	25	26 You want to keep these dates free. Make excuses.	27	28 dinner for Dad's birthday	29 go dancing with Jess & Bo	30 You might have a date. Give an excuse.

B **PAIR WORK** Now work with another student. Discuss the excuses your partner gave you in Part A. Decide which excuses were probably true and which ones were probably not true.

A: Pablo said that on the 7th he had to take care of his neighbors' cats. That was probably not true.
B: I agree. I think . . .

INTERCHANGE 15 Tough choices

A What would you do in each of these situations? Circle **a**, **b**, or **c**.
If you think you would do something else, write your suggestion next to **d**.

1. If I saw someone shoplifting in a store, I would . . .
   a. pretend I didn't notice.
   b. talk to the store manager.
   c. talk to the shoplifter.
   d. _____.

2. If I saw an elderly woman trying to cross a street, I would . . .
   a. keep walking.
   b. offer to help.
   c. try to stop traffic for her.
   d. _____.

3. If I saw someone standing on a highway next to a car with smoke coming from the engine, I would . . .
   a. continue driving.
   b. stop and help.
   c. use my cell phone to call the police.
   d. _____.

4. If I saw my friend's boyfriend or girlfriend with someone other than my friend, I would . . .
   a. say nothing.
   b. talk to my friend.
   c. talk to my friend's boyfriend or girlfriend.
   d. _____.

5. If I were eating dinner in a restaurant and I found a hair in my food, I would . . .
   a. remove it and continue eating.
   b. mention it to the server.
   c. demand to speak to the manager.
   d. _____.

B **GROUP WORK** Compare your choices for each situation in part A.

A: What would you do if you saw someone shoplifting in a store?
B: I'm not sure. Maybe I would pretend I didn't notice.
C: Really? I wouldn't. I would . . .

C **CLASS ACTIVITY** Take a class survey. Find out which choice was most popular for each situation. Talk about any other suggestions people added for **d**.

INTERCHANGE 16B Just a bunch of excuses

Student B

A **PAIR WORK** You and your partner want to get together. Ask and answer questions to find a day when you are both free. You also want to keep time open for other friends, so give excuses for those days. Write your partner's excuses on the calendar.

A: Do you want to meet on the 2nd?
B: I'm sorry. I'm going to an engagement party. Are you free on the 1st?
A: Well, I . . .

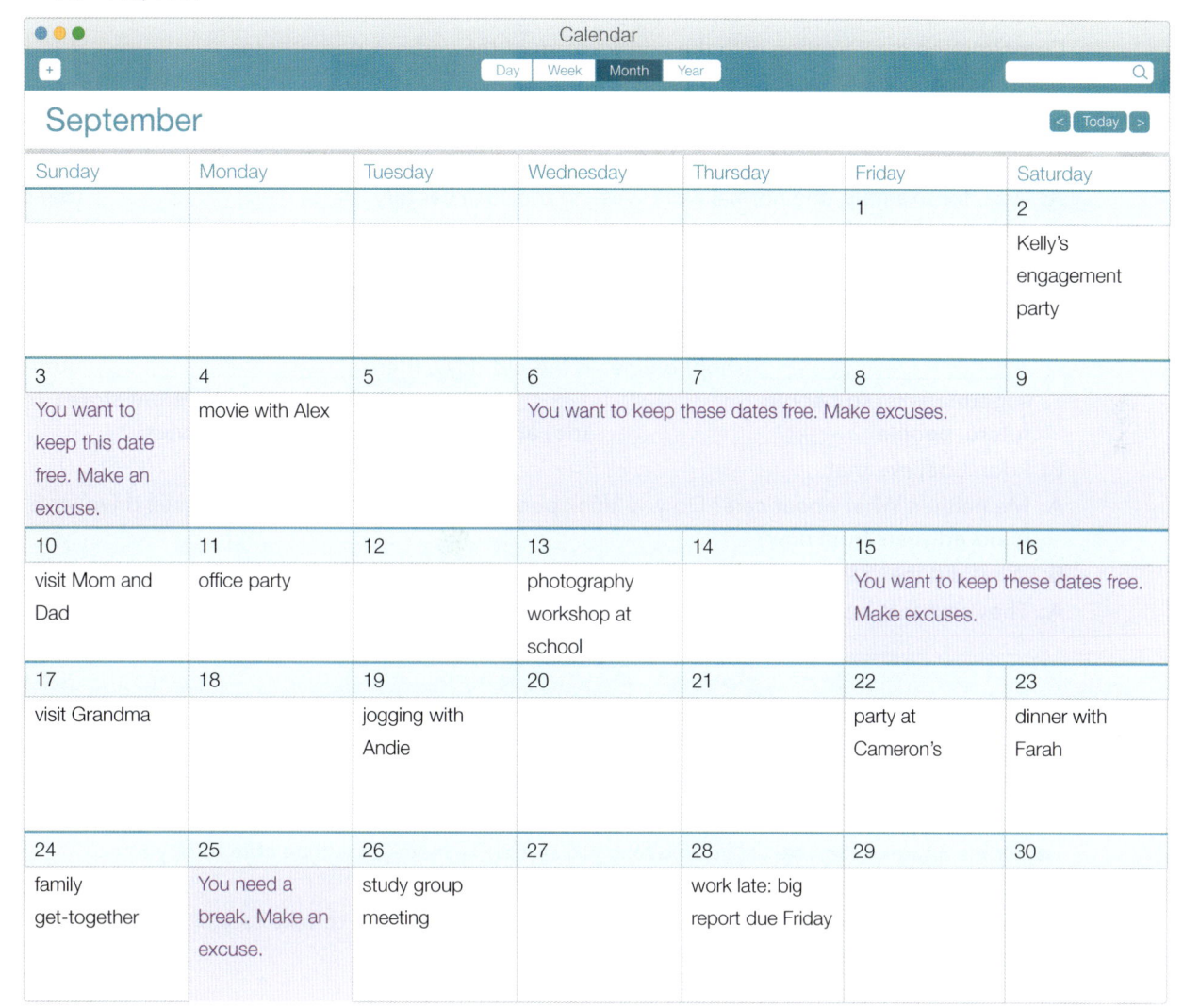

Calendar — September

Sunday	Monday	Tuesday	Wednesday	Thursday	Friday	Saturday
					1	2 Kelly's engagement party
3 You want to keep this date free. Make an excuse.	4 movie with Alex	5	6 You want to keep these dates free. Make excuses.	7	8	9
10 visit Mom and Dad	11 office party	12	13 photography workshop at school	14	15 You want to keep these dates free. Make excuses.	16
17 visit Grandma	18	19 jogging with Andie	20	21	22 party at Cameron's	23 dinner with Farah
24 family get-together	25 You need a break. Make an excuse.	26 study group meeting	27	28 work late: big report due Friday	29	30

B **PAIR WORK** Now work with another student. Discuss the excuses your partner gave you in Part A. Decide which excuses were probably true and which ones were probably not true.

A: Maria said that on the 9th she had to help her brother paint his kitchen. That might be true.
B: I agree. I think . . .

Grammar plus

UNIT 9

1 Time contrasts — page 59

> ■ Use the modal *might* to say something is possible in the present or future: In a few years, movie theaters **might** not exist. = In a few years, maybe movie theaters won't exist.

Complete the conversation with the correct form of the verbs in parentheses.
Use the past, present, or future tense.

A: I saw a fascinating program last night. It talked about the past, the present, and the future.
B: What kinds of things did it describe?
A: Well, for example, the normal work week in the 19th century _____ (be) over 60 hours. Nowadays, many people _____ (work) around 40 hours a week.
B: Well, that sounds like progress.
A: You're right. But on the show, they said that most people _____ (work) fewer hours in the future. They also talked about the way we shop. These days, many of us _____ (shop) online. In the old days, there _____ (be) no supermarkets, so people _____ (have to) go to a lot of different stores. In the future, people _____ (do) all their shopping from their phones.
B: I don't believe that.
A: Me neither. What about cars? Do you think people _____ (still drive) cars a hundred years from now?
B: What did they say on the show?
A: They said that before the car, people _____ (walk) everywhere. Nowadays, we _____ (drive) everywhere. And that _____ (not change).

2 Conditional sentences with *if* clauses — page 61

> ■ The *if* clause can come before or after the main clause: **If** I change my eating habits, I'll feel healthier./I'll feel healthier **if** I change my eating habits. Always use a comma when the *if* clause comes before the main clause.
> ■ For the future of *can*, use *will be able to*: If you save some money, you**'ll be able to buy** a car.
> (NOT: . . . you'll can buy a car.)
> ■ For the future of *must*, use *will have to*: If you get a dog, you**'ll have to take care** of it.
> (NOT: . . . you'll must take care of it.)

Complete the sentences with the correct form of the verbs in parentheses.

1. If you ___exercise___ (exercise) more often, you' __ll feel__ (feel) more energetic.
2. If you _____ (join) a gym, exercise _____ (become) part of your routine.
3. You _____ (not have to) worry about staying in shape if you _____ (work out) three or four times a week.
4. If you _____ (ride) a bike or _____ (run) a few times a week, you _____ (lose) weight and _____ (gain) muscle.
5. You _____ (sleep) better at night if you _____ (exercise) regularly.
6. If you _____ (start) exercising, you _____ (might/not have) as many colds and other health problems.

UNIT 10

1 Gerunds; short responses (page 65)

- Short responses with *so* and *neither* are ways of agreeing. The subject (noun or pronoun) comes after the verb: I love traveling. So **do I**. (NOT: So I do.) I can't stand talking on the phone. Neither **can I**. (NOT: Neither I can.)

Rewrite A's line using the words given. Then write an agreement for B.

1. I hate working alone. (can't stand)
   A: <u>I can't stand working alone.</u>
   B: <u>Neither can I.</u>
2. I don't like reading about politics or politicians. (interested in)
   A: _____
   B: _____
3. I can solve problems. (good at)
   A: _____
   B: _____
4. I have no problem with working on weekends. (don't mind)
   A: _____
   B: _____
5. I love learning new things. (enjoy)
   A: _____
   B: _____
6. I can't develop new ideas. (not good at)
   A: _____
   B: _____

2 Clauses with *because* (page 68)

- Clauses with *because* answer the question "Why?" or "Why not?": Why would you make a good flight attendant? I'd make a good flight attendant **because** I love traveling, and I'm good with people.

Complete the sentences with *because* and the phrases in the box.

> I don't write very well
> I love arguing with people
> I'm afraid of flying
> ✓ I'm much too short
> I'm not patient enough to work with kids
> I'm really bad with numbers

1. I could never be a fashion model <u>because I'm much too short</u>.
2. I wouldn't make a good high school teacher _____.
3. I wouldn't want to be a flight attendant _____.
4. I could never be an accountant _____.
5. I would make a bad journalist _____.
6. I'd be an excellent lawyer _____.

Unit 10 Grammar plus 141

UNIT 11

1 Passive with *by* (simple past) — page 73

- The past participle of regular verbs is the same form as the simple past: Leonardo da Vinci **painted** *Mona Lisa* in 1503. *Mona Lisa* was **painted** by Leonardo da Vinci in 1503.
- The past participle of some – but not all – irregular verbs is the same form as the simple past: The Egyptians **built** the Pyramids. The Pyramids were **built** by the Egyptians. BUT Jane Austen **wrote** *Pride and Prejudice*. *Pride and Prejudice* was **written** by Jane Austen.

Change the sentences from active to passive with *by*.

1. The Chinese invented paper around 100 C.E.
   Paper was invented by the Chinese around 100 C.E.
2. Marie Curie discovered radium in 1898.
   _____
3. Dr. Felix Hoffmann made the first aspirin in 1899.
   _____
4. Tim Berners-Lee developed the World Wide Web in 1989.
   _____
5. William Herschel identified the planet Uranus in 1781.
   _____
6. Georges Bizet wrote the opera *Carmen* in the 1870s.
   _____

2 Passive without *by* (simple present) — page 75

- When it is obvious or not important who is doing the action, don't use a *by* phrase: Both the Olympics and the World Cup are held every four years. (NOT: . . . are held by people . . .)

Complete the information with *is* or *are* and the past participle of the verbs in the box.

base	know
export	✓ speak
import	use

1. Portuguese – not Spanish – _is spoken_____ in Brazil.
2. Diamonds and gold from South Africa _____ by countries all over the world.
3. The U.S. dollar _____ in Puerto Rico.
4. Colombia _____ for its delicious coffee.
5. Many electronic products _____ by Japan and South Korea. It's an important industry for these two countries.
6. The economy in many island countries, such as Jamaica, _____ on tourism.

UNIT 12

1 Past continuous vs. simple past — page 79

> ■ When the past continuous is used with the simple past, both actions happened at the same time, but the past continuous action started earlier. The simple past action interrupted the past continuous action.
>
> Earlier action — 6:00 — *I was watching TV*
> Later action — 6:20 — *when the phone rang.*

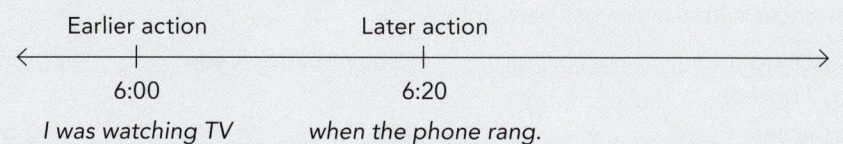

Complete the conversations with the correct form of the verbs in parentheses. Use the past continuous or the simple past.

1. **A:** What happened to you?
   B: I ____*fell*____ (fall) while I ____*was jogging*____ (jog) in the park.
2. **A:** _____ you _____ (see) the storm yesterday?
   B: Yes! It _____ (start) while I _____ (drive) to work.
3. **A:** We finally _____ (move) to a larger apartment.
   B: That's good. I know you _____ (live) in a tiny place when your daughter _____ (be) born.
4. **A:** My sister _____ (have) a bad accident. She _____ (hurt) her back when she _____ (lift) weights at the gym.
   B: That _____ (happen) to me last year, but I _____ (not lift) weights. I _____ (take) a boxing class, and I _____ (trip).

2 Present perfect continuous — page 81

> ■ The same time expressions used with the present perfect can also be used with the present perfect continuous. Don't confuse *for* and *since*: I've been working here **for** 5 years./I've been working here **since** 2010.

Complete the sentences with the present perfect continuous form of the verbs in parentheses.

1. **A:** What ____*have*____ you ____*been doing*____ all day?
   B: I _____ (clean) the house, and Peter _____ (watch) TV. He _____ (not feel) very well lately.
   A: How _____ you _____ (feel) these days?
   B: I _____ (feel) great. I _____ (not eat) any junk food, and I _____ (exercise) a lot. I _____ (take) really good care of myself.
2. **A:** How long _____ you and Joe _____ (date)?
   B: We _____ (go out) together for almost a year. Can you believe it?
   A: Maya and I _____ (date) for even longer. I think it's time to get married. We _____ (talk) about it a lot lately.
   B: Joe and I _____ (not talk) about marriage, but I _____ (think) about it.

UNIT 13

1 Participles as adjectives — page 87

> ■ Adjectives ending in –ing are present participles. They are things that *cause* a feeling. Adjectives ending in –ed are past participles. They *express* the feeling.

Complete the sentences with the correct participle.

1. Why are we watching this ____boring____ movie? Aren't you ____bored____ with it? (boring / bored)
2. Kristen Stewart is an _____ actress. I'm _____ by her talent. (amazing / amazed)
3. Are you _____ in computer-generated special effects? The latest 3-D movies are very _____. (interesting / interested)
4. I had an _____ experience the last time I went to the movies. I started to cough, and I couldn't stop. I was really _____. (embarrassing / embarrassed)
5. Julie and I saw an Italian comedy yesterday. I found it _____, but Julie didn't seem very _____ by it. (amusing / amused)
6. Oh, I'm really _____ with Jeremy right now. He took me to the most _____ movie last night. I wanted to walk out after half an hour, but he wouldn't leave! (disgusting / disgusted)
7. Do you think sci-fi movie directors make their films _____ intentionally? I get so _____ by the complicated storylines and weird characters. (confusing / confused)
8. I think that great books make great movies. If I find a book _____, I'm usually _____ by the movie, too. (fascinating / fascinated)

2 Relative pronouns for people and things — page 89

> ■ Relative clauses give information about nouns. Don't use a personal pronoun in a relative clause: He's an actor **that** won two Oscars. (NOT: He's an actor that ~~he~~ won two Oscars.)

Complete the conversations. Use *that* for things and *who* for people.

A: How did you like the movie last night? Was it any good?
B: It wasn't bad, but it's not the kind of movie ____that____ makes you think. I like films _____ have a strong message and interesting storylines.
A: How about the acting? Did you like the actors _____ star in it?
B: Jessica Biel is pretty good, actually.
A: Oh, she's that beautiful actress _____ is married to Justin Timberlake.
B: Justin who? Who's that?
A: Oh, you know him. He's the one _____ was in the band 'NSync years ago. It was a "boy band" _____ was popular in the 1990s.
B: I remember 'NSync, but I don't remember the names of the guys _____ were in the band.
A: Well, I loved Justin Timberlake when I was a kid. And he's not a bad actor. Did you see the movie *The Social Network*?
B: I did see that. It's about the guys _____ started Facebook, right? I didn't realize Justin Timberlake was in it. Now I'll have to see it again!

UNIT 14

1 Modals and adverbs page 93

> - Use the modals *might/may*, *could*, and *must* and the adverbs *maybe/perhaps*, *probably*, and *definitely* when you aren't sure about what you're saying:
> Slight possibility: *might, may, maybe, perhaps*
> Possibility: *could, probably*
> Strong possibility: *must, definitely*

Rewrite each sentence in different ways, using the words in parentheses.

1. Perhaps it means she doesn't agree with you.
   a. (maybe) <u>Maybe it means she doesn't agree with you.</u>
   b. (might) _____
   c. (may) _____
2. That gesture could mean, "Come here."
   a. (probably) _____
3. That almost definitely means he doesn't understand you.
   a. (must) _____

2 Permission, obligation, and prohibition page 95

> - Use *have/has* with *got to*: You**'ve got to** keep the door closed. (NOT: You ~~got to~~ keep the door closed.)

Complete the conversations with the words and phrases in the box.
Use each word or phrase only once.

are allowed to	✓ can't
aren't allowed to	have to
can	have got to

1. **A:** Oh, no! That sign says, "No fishing." That means we _____can't_____ fish here.
   B: You're right. We _____ go somewhere else to fish. I think you _____ fish in the pond on Cedar Road. Let's go there.
2. **A:** What does that sign mean?
   B: It means bad news for us. It means you _____ bring dogs to the beach. We'd better take Buddy home.
3. **A:** Please don't leave your garbage here. You _____ put it in the trash room down the hall. That's one of the building's rules.
   B: I'm really sorry.
4. **A:** You _____ put your bike in the bike room downstairs, if you want. It's much safer than locking it up outside.
   B: Oh, that's great! I'll do that. I didn't know about the bike room.

UNIT 15

1 Unreal conditional sentences with if clauses — page 101

> ■ The clauses in unreal conditional sentences can come in either order. Don't use a comma when the *if* clause comes second: **If** I won the lottery, I'd share the money with my family./I'd share the money with my family **if** I won the lottery.

Complete the conversation with the correct form of the verbs in parentheses.

1. **A:** If a friend _____ (ask) to borrow some money, what _____ you _____ (say)?
   B: Well, if I _____ (have) any extra money that month, I _____ probably _____ (give) it to her.

2. **A:** What _____ you _____ (do) if someone _____ (give) you a million dollars?
   B: Hmm, I'm not sure. I _____ (buy) a lot of nice clothes and jewelry, or I _____ (spend) some and _____ (give) some away, or I _____ (put) it all in the bank.

3. **A:** If you _____ (think) a friend was doing something dangerous, _____ you _____ (say) something to him, or _____ you _____ (keep) quiet?
   B: I _____ definitely _____ (talk) to my friend about it.

4. **A:** What _____ you _____ (do) if you _____ (have) a problem with your boss?
   B: That's a hard one. If that _____ (happen), I _____ (talk) to the human resources department about it, or I _____ just _____ (sit down) with my boss and _____ (talk) about the situation.

2 Past modals — page 103

> ■ Use *should have* and *would have* for all subjects. They don't change form: He **should have called** sooner. (NOT: He should has called sooner.)

Read the situations. Use the words in parentheses to write opinions and suggestions.

1. My neighbor had a party last night. It was very loud, so I called the police.
   (you / speak / to your neighbor first)
   <u>You should have spoken to your neighbor first.</u>

2. The mail carrier put someone else's mail in my box. I threw it away.
   (you / write / a note and leave / the mail in your box)
   _____

3. My sister asked if I liked her new dress. It didn't look good on her, but I said it did.
   (I / tell her the truth)
   _____

4. A salesperson called me last night. I didn't want to buy anything, but I let her talk to me for almost half an hour.
   (I / tell her I'm not interested / hang up)
   _____

UNIT 16

1 Reported speech: requests — page 107

> ■ When a reported request is negative, *not* comes before *to*: Don't leave your wet towel on the floor. She told me **not to leave** my wet towel on the floor.
> (NOT: She told me to not leave my wet towel on the floor.)

Harry's roommate, Tyler, is making some requests. Read what Tyler said to Harry. Write the requests with the verbs in parentheses and reported speech.

1. "Can you put away your clean clothes?" (ask)
   Tyler asked Harry to put away his clean clothes.

2. "Meet me in the cafeteria at school at noon." (say)

3. "Don't leave your shoes in the living room." (tell)

4. "Hang up your wet towels." (say)

5. "Could you stop using my phone?" (ask)

6. "Make your bed on weekdays." (tell)

7. "Don't eat my food." (say)

8. "Be a better roommate!" (tell)

2 Reported speech: statements — page 109

> ■ The tense of the introducing verb (*ask, say, tell*) changes when the sentence is reported: simple present → simple past; present continuous → past continuous; present perfect → past perfect. Modals change, too: *can* → *could*; *will* → *would*; *may* → *might*.

Bill and Kathy are having a barbecue on Sunday. They're upset because a lot of their friends can't come. Read what their friends said. Change the excuses into reported speech.

1. Lori: "I have to visit my grandparents that day."
   Lori said that she had to visit her grandparents that day.

2. Mario: "I'm going to a play on Sunday."

3. Julia: "I've promised to take my brother to the movies that day."

4. Daniel: "I can't come. I have to study for a huge exam on Monday."

5. The neighbors: "We'll be out of town all weekend."

6. Alice: "I may have to babysit my nephew."

Grammar plus answer key

Unit 9

1 Time contrasts
A: I saw a fascinating program last night. It talked about the past, the present, and the future.
B: What kinds of things did it describe?
A: Well, for example, the normal work week in the 19th century **was/used to be** over 60 hours. Nowadays, many people **work/are working** around 40 hours a week.
B: Well, that sounds like progress.
A: You're right. But on the show, they said that most people **will work/might work** fewer hours in the future. They also talked about the way we shop. These days, many of us **shop** online. In the old days, there **were** no supermarkets, so people **had to go/used to have to go** to a lot of different stores. In the future, people **will do/might do/are going to do** all their shopping from their phones.
B: I don't believe that.
A: Me neither. What about cars? Do you think people **will still drive/are still going to drive** cars a hundred years from now?
B: What did they say on the show?
A: They said that before the car, people **walked/used to walk** everywhere. Nowadays, we **drive** everywhere. And that **won't change/isn't going to change/'s not going to change**.

2 Conditional sentences with *if* clauses
2. If you **join** a gym, exercise **will become** part of your routine.
3. You **won't have to** worry about staying in shape if you **work out** three or four times a week.
4. If you **ride** a bike or **run** a few times a week, you**'ll lose** weight and **gain** muscle.
5. You**'ll sleep** better at night if you **exercise** regularly.
6. If you **start** exercising, you **might not have** as many colds and other health problems.

Unit 10

1 Gerunds; short responses
2. A: I'm not interested in reading about politics or politicians.
   B: Neither am I.
3. A: I'm good at solving problems.
   B: So am I.
4. A: I don't mind working on weekends.
   B: Neither do I.
5. A: I enjoy learning new things.
   B: So do I.
6. A: I'm not good at developing new ideas.
   B: Neither am I.

2 Clauses with *because*
2. I wouldn't make a good high school teacher **because I'm not patient enough to work with kids**.
3. I wouldn't want to be a flight attendant **because I'm afraid of flying**.
4. I could never be an accountant **because I'm really bad with numbers**.
5. I would make a bad journalist **because I don't write very well**.
6. I'd be an excellent lawyer **because I love arguing with people**.

Unit 11

1 Passive with *by* (simple past)
2. Radium was discovered by Marie Curie in 1898.
3. The first aspirin was made by Dr. Felix Hoffmann in 1899.
4. The World Wide Web was developed by Tim Berners-Lee in 1989.
5. The planet Uranus was identified in 1781 by William Herschel.
6. The opera *Carmen* was written by Georges Bizet in the 1870s.

2 Passive without *by* (simple present)
2. Diamonds and gold from South Africa **are imported** by countries all over the world.
3. The U.S. dollar **is used** in Puerto Rico.
4. Colombia **is known** for its delicious coffee.
5. Many electronic products **are exported** by Japan and Korea. It's an important industry for these two countries.
6. The economy in many island countries, such as Jamaica, **is based** on tourism.

Unit 12

1 Past continuous vs. simple past
2. A: **Did** you **see** the storm yesterday?
   B: Yes! It **started** while I **was driving** to work.
3. A: We finally **moved** to a larger apartment.
   B: That's good. I know you **were living** in a tiny place when your daughter **was** born.
4. A: My sister **had** a bad accident. She **hurt** her back when she **was lifting** weights at the gym.
   B: That **happened** to me last year, but I **wasn't lifting** weights. I **was taking** a boxing class, and I **tripped**.

2 Present perfect continuous
1. A: What **have** you **been doing** all day?
   B: I**'ve been cleaning** the house, and Peter **has been watching** TV. He **hasn't been feeling** very well lately.
   A: How **have** you **been feeling** these days?
   B: I**'ve been feeling** great. I **haven't been eating** any junk food, and I**'ve been exercising** a lot. I**'ve been taking** really good care of myself.
2. A: How long **have** you and Joe **been dating**?
   B: We**'ve been going out** together for almost a year. Can you believe it?
   A: Maya and I **have been dating** for even longer. I think it's time to get married. We**'ve been talking** about it a lot lately.
   B: Joe and I **haven't been talking** about marriage, but I**'ve been thinking** about it.

Unit 13

1 Participles as adjectives
2. Kristen Stewart is an **amazing** actress. I'm **amazed** by her talent.
3. Are you **interested** in computer-generated special effects? The latest 3-D movies are very **interesting**.
4. I had an **embarrassing** experience the last time I went to the movies. I started to cough, and I couldn't stop. I was really **embarrassed**.
5. Julie and I saw an Italian comedy yesterday. I found it **amusing**, but Julie didn't seem very **amused** by it.
6. Oh, I'm really **disgusted** with Jeremy right now. He took me to the most **disgusting** movie last night. I wanted to walk out after half an hour, but he wouldn't leave!
7. Do you think sci-fi movie directors make their films **confusing** intentionally? I get so **confused** by the complicated storylines and weird characters.
8. I think that great books make great movies. If I find a book **fascinating**, I'm usually **fascinated** by the movie, too.

2 Relative pronouns for people and things
A: How did you like the movie last night? Was it any good?
B: It wasn't bad, but it's not the kind of movie **that** makes you think. I like films **that** have a strong message and interesting storylines.
A: How about the acting? Did you like the actors **who** star in it?
B: Jessica Biel is pretty good, actually.
A: Oh, she's that beautiful actress **who** is married to Justin Timberlake.
B: Justin who? Who's that?
A: Oh, you know him. He's the one **who** was in the band 'NSync years ago. It was a "boy band" **that** was popular in the 1990s.
B: I remember 'NSync, but I don't remember the names of the guys **who** were in the band.
A: Well, I loved Justin Timberlake when I was a kid. And he's not a bad actor. Did you see the movie *The Social Network*?
B: I did see that. It's about the guys **who** started Facebook, right? I didn't realize Justin Timberlake was in it. Now I'll have to see it again!

Unit 14

1 Modals and adverbs
1. a. Maybe it means she doesn't agree with you.
   b. It might mean she doesn't agree with you.
   c. It may mean she doesn't agree with you.
2. a. That gesture probably means, "Come here."
3. a. That must mean he doesn't understand you.

2 Permission, obligation, and prohibition
1. A: Oh, no! That sign says, "No fishing." That means we **can't** fish here.
   B: You're right. We**'ve got to/have to** go somewhere else to fish. I think you**'re allowed to/can** fish in the pond on Cedar Road. Let's go there.
2. A: What does that sign mean?
   B: It means bad news for us. It means you **aren't allowed to** bring dogs to the beach. We'd better take Buddy home.
3. A: Please don't leave your garbage here. You**'ve got to/have to** put it in the trash room down the hall. That's one of the building's rules.
   B: I'm really sorry.
4. A: You **can** put your bike in the bike room downstairs, if you want. It's much safer than locking it up outside.
   B: Oh, that's great! I'll do that. I didn't know about the bike room.

Unit 15

1 Unreal conditional sentences with *if* clauses
1. A: If a friend **asked** to borrow some money, what **would** you **say**?
   B: Well, if I **had** any extra money that month, I **would** probably **give** it to her.
2. A: What **would/could** you **do** if someone **gave** you a million dollars?
   B: Hmm, I'm not sure. I **could/might buy** a lot of nice clothes and jewelry, or I **could/might spend** some and **give** some away, or I **could/might put** it all in the bank.
3. A: If you **thought** a friend was doing something dangerous, **would** you **say** something to him, or **would** you **keep** quiet?
   B: I **would** definitely **talk** to my friend about it.
4. A: What **would** you **do** if you **had** a problem with your boss?
   B: That's a hard one. If that **happened, I might/could talk** to the human resources department about it, or I **might/could** just **sit down** with my boss and **talk** about the situation.

2 Past modals
2. You should have written a note and left the mail in your box.
3. I would have told her the truth.
4. I would have told her I wasn't interested and hung up (the phone).

Unit 16

1 Reported speech: requests
2. Tyler said to meet him in the cafeteria at school at noon.
3. Tyler told him/Harry not to leave his shoes in the living room.
4. Tyler said to hang up his wet towels.
5. Tyler asked him/Harry to stop using his/Tyler's phone.
6. Tyler told him/Harry to make his bed on weekdays.
7. Tyler said not to eat his/Tyler's food.
8. Tyler told him/Harry to be a better roommate.

2 Reported speech: statements
1. Lori said (that) she had to visit her grandparents that day.
   Lori told them (that) she had to visit her grandparents that day.
2. Mario said/told them (that) he was going to a play on Sunday.
3. Julia said/told them (that) she had promised to take her brother to the movies that day.
4. Daniel said/told them (that) he couldn't come because he had to study for a huge exam on Monday.
5. The neighbors said/told them (that) they would be out of town all weekend.
6. Alice said/told them (that) she might have to babysit her nephew.

Grammar plus answer key

Credits

The authors and publishers acknowledge the following sources of copyright material and are grateful for the permissions granted. While every effort has been made, it has not always been possible to identify the sources of all the material used, or to trace all copyright holders. If any omissions are brought to our notice, we will be happy to include the appropriate acknowledgements on reprinting and in the next update to the digital edition, as applicable.

Texts
Text on p. 83 adapted from "Deaf band 'Beethoven's Nightmare' feels the music" by Dennis McCarthy. Copyright © Los Angeles Daily News. Reproduced with permission.

Key: B = Below, BC = Below Centre, BL = Below Left, BR = Below Right, B/G = Background, C = Centre, CL = Centre Left, CR = Centre Right, L = Left, R = Right, T = Top, TC = Top Centre, TL = Top Left, TR = Top Right.

Illustrations
337 Jon (KJA Artists): 39, 92(B), 97; **Mark Duffin**: 18, 25(C), 37, 43(T); **Pablo Gallego** (Beehive Illustration): 43(B); **Thomas Girard** (Good Illustration): 2, 22, 41, 93; **John Goodwin** (Eye Candy Illustration): 40; **Daniel Gray**: 75, 118, 120; **Quino Marin** (The Organisation): 36, 80, 128; **Gavin Reece** (New Division): 58, 81, 119; **Paul Williams** (Sylvie Poggio Artists): 16, 114.

Photos
Back cover (woman with whiteboard): Jenny Acheson/Stockbyte/GettyImages; Back cover (whiteboard): Nemida/GettyImages; Back cover (man using phone): Betsie Van Der Meer/Taxi/GettyImages; Back cover (woman smiling): PeopleImages.com/DigitalVision/GettyImages; Back cover (name tag): Tetra Images/GettyImages; Back cover (handshake): David Lees/Taxi/GettyImages; p. v (TL): Hero Images/Getty Images; p. v (TR): Cultura RM Exclusive/dotdotred/Getty Images; p. v (CL): vitchanan/iStock/Getty Images Plus/Getty Images; p. v (CR): Svetlana Braun/iStock/Getty Images Plus/Getty Images; p. v (BL): Hero Images/Getty Images; p. v (BR): Cultura RM Exclusive/dotdotred/Getty Images; p. vi (Unit 9), p. 58 (header): Artur Debat/Moment/Getty Images; p. 58 (TL): Michael Fresco/Evening Standard/Hulton Archive/Getty Images; p. 58 (TC): Car Culture/Car Culture ® Collection/Getty Images; p. 58 (TR): Javier Pierini/The Image Bank/Getty Images; p. 59: Hero Images/Getty Images; p. 60 (CR): Jordan Siemens/Iconica/Getty Images; p. 60 (BR): RoBeDeRo/E+/Getty Images; p. 61: GH-Images/iStock/Getty Images Plus/Getty Images; p. 62 (TR): Barry Austin Photography/Iconica/Getty Images; p. 62 (Ex 11a: photo 1): Hill Street Studios/Blend Images/Getty Images; p. 62 (Ex 11a: photo 2): Hill Street Studios/Blend Images/Getty Images; p. 62 (Ex 11a: photo 3): Hill Street Studios/Blend Images/Getty Images; p. 62 (Ex 11a: photo 4): Aziz Ary Neto/Cultura/Getty Images; p. 62 (Ex 11a: photo 5): Blend Images-Mike Kemp/Brand X Pictures/Getty Images; p. 63: Daniel Schoenen/LOOK-foto/LOOK/Getty Images; p. vi (Unit 10), p. 64 (header): Hero Images/Getty Images; p. 64 (BR): BJI/Blue Jean Images/Getty Images; p. 65: Caiaimage/Paul Bradbury/Caiaimage/Getty Images; p. 67 (disorganised): Stuart McCall/Photographer's Choice/Getty Images; p. 67 (hardworking): Dave and Les Jacobs/Blend Images/Getty Images; p. 67 (Ex 9a): adventtr/E+/Getty Images; p. 67 (Paula): Portra Images/Taxi/Getty Images; p. 67 (Shawn): PeopleImages/DigitalVision/Getty Images; p. 67 (Dalia): Jetta Productions/Blend Images/Getty Images; p. 68: Hill Street Studios/Getty Images; p. 69: Image Source/Getty Images; p. 71: monkeybusinessimages/iStock/Getty Images Plus/Getty Images; p. vi (Unit 11), p. 72 (header): d3sign/Moment/Getty Images; p. 72 (Eiffel Tower): Kart Thomas/Photolibrary/Getty Images; p. 72 (Machu Picchu): mimmopellicola.com/Moment/Getty Images; p. 72 (Neuschwanstein Castle): Brian Lawrence/Getty Images; p. 72 (Mount Fuji): Christian Kober/robertharding/Getty Images; p. 72 (Statue of Liberty): Brian Lawrence/Getty Images; p. 72 (Big Ben): Joe Fox/Photographer's Choice/Getty Images; p. 73: Print Collector/Hulton Fine Art Collection/Getty Images; p. 74 (L): JTB Photo/Universal Images Group/Getty Images; p. 74 (C): PIERRE VERDY/AFP Creative/Getty Images; p. 74 (R): JLGutierrez/iStock/Getty Images Plus/Getty Images; p. 76 (TR): Radius Images/Getty Images Plus/Getty Images; p. 76 (CR): Jodi Jacobson/E+/Getty Images; p. 76 (BR): Photography Aubrey Stoll/Moment/Getty Images; p. 77 (TL): Hemant Chawla/The India Today Group/Getty Images; p. 77 (CR): Luis Javier Sandoval/Oxford Scientific/Getty Images; p. 77 (BL): EPA european pressphoto agency b.v./Alamy; p. vi (Unit 12), p. 78 (header): Timur Emek/Getty Images Europe/Getty Images; p. 78 (TL): JasnaXX/RooM/Getty Images; p. 78 (TR): Rodrigo Alvarez-Icaza/Moment Open/Getty Images; p. 78 (BR): James Woodson/Photodisc/Getty Images; p. 79 (TR): Michael Krinke/Vetta/Getty Images; p. 79 (BR): biglike/iStock/Getty Images Plus/Getty Images; p. 82: David Lees/Taxi/Getty Images; p. 83: Rachel Murray/WireImage/Getty Images; p. 84: Ben Pruchnie/Getty Images Europe/Getty Images; p. vi (Unit 13), p. 86 (header): spawns/iStock/Getty Images Plus/Getty Images; p. 86 (TL): Jim Spellman/WireImage/Getty Images; p. 86 (TR): Pictorial Press Ltd/Alamy; p. 86 (BR): Murray Close/Contributor/Moviepix/GettyImages; p. 87: Araya Diaz/WireImage/Getty Image; p. 89: Jon Kopaloff/FilmMagic/Getty Images; p. 90 (TR): Daniel Zuchnik/WireImage/Getty Images; p. 90 (BR): Valerie Macon/Getty Images North America/Getty Images; p. 91 (BL): Paul Hawthorne/Getty Images North America/Getty Images; p. 91 (TR): Alberto E. Rodriguez/Getty Images North America/Getty Images; p. vi (Unit 14), p. 92 (header): Joe Drivas/Photographer's Choice/Getty Images; p. 93 (Ex 4: photo 1): champja/iStock/Getty Images Plus/Getty Images; p. 93 (Ex 4: photo 2): Dahl Per/Getty Images; p. 93 (Ex 4: photo 3): Seymour Hewitt/The Image Bank/Getty Images; p. 93 (Ex 4: photo 4): Merbe/E+/Getty Images; p. 93 (Ex 4: photo 5): BJI/Blue Jean Images/Getty Images; p. 93 (Ex 4: photo 6): m-imagephotography/iStock/Getty Images Plus/Getty Images; p. 94: BJI/Blue Jean Images/Getty Images; p. 98: uniquely india/Getty Images; p. 99: GlobalStock/E+/Getty Images; p. vi (Unit 15), p. 100 (header): Tetra Images/Getty Images; p. 100 (TL): moodboard/Brand X Pictures/Getty Images; p. 100 (CL): Marcin Balcerzak/Hemera/Getty Images Plus/Getty Images; p. 100 (C): Erik Dreyer/The Image Bank/Getty Images; p. 100 (BR): Thomas_EyeDesign/E+/Getty Images; p. 102: pp76/iStock/Getty Images Plus/Getty Images; p. 104 (TR): Wavebreakmedia Ltd/Wavebreak Media/Getty Images Plus/Getty Images; p. 104 (CR): Ariel Skelley/Blend Images/Getty Images Plus/Getty Images; p. 105 (Jack): Frank Herholdt/The Image Bank/Getty Images; p. 105 (Sarah): Betsie Van Der Meer/Taxi/Getty Images; p. 105 (Maya): Caiaimage/Sam Edwards/Caiaimage/Getty Images; p. 105 (Dag): Dimitri Otis/Taxi/Getty Images; p. 105 (Andres): Ridofranz/iStock/Getty Images Plus/Getty Images; p. 105 (Marta): Mark Edward Atkinson/Tracey Lee/Blend Images/Getty Images; p. vi (Unit 16), p. 106 (header): Dan Dumitru Comaniciu/iStock/Getty Images Plus/Getty Images; p. 106 (TR): GK Hart/Vikki Hart/Stone/Getty Images; p. 107: ajr_images/iStock/Getty Images Plus/Getty Images; p. 108 (Gabriel): gradyreese/E+/Getty Images; p. 108 (Craig): Leland Bobbe/Image Source/Getty Images; p. 109 (Grant): Ezra Bailey/Taxi/Getty Images; p. 109 (Sayo): Sappington Todd/Getty Images; p. 109 (Diego): Fuse/Getty Images; p. 109 (Carrie): Jordan Siemens/Getty Images; p. 110: Jamie Grill/Photodisc/Getty Images; p. 111 (TR): Tom Le Goff/DigitalVision/Getty Images; p. 111 (CR): Ugurhan Betin/iStock/Getty Images Plus/Getty Images; p. 112: Moodboard Stock Photography Ltd./Canopy/Getty Images; p. 123 (Ex a.1): Hero Images/Getty Images; p. 123 (Ex a.2): Kontrec/E+/Getty Images; p. 123 (Ex a.3): Robert Daly/Caiaimage/Getty Images; p. 123 (Ex a.4): quavondo/E+/Getty Images; p. 123 (Ex a.5): Wavebreakmedia Ltd/Wavebreak Media/Getty Images Plus/Getty Images; p. 123 (Ex a.6): Wendy Connett/Moment/Getty Images; p. 123 (Ex a.7): Dimitri Otis/DigitalVision/Getty Images; p. 123 (Ex a.8): Justin Pumfrey/Iconica/Getty Images; p. 123 (Ex a.9): monkeybusinessimages/iStock/Getty Images Plus/Getty Images; p. 123 (Ex a.10): Alberto Guglielmi/The Image Bank/Getty Images; p. 124: opolja/iStock/Getty Images Plus/Getty Images; p. 125 (B/G): CSA Images/Printstock Collection/Getty Images; p. 126 (TL): blackred/E+/Getty Images; p. 126 (TR): blackred/E+/Getty Images; p. 126 (B/G): Nathaniel Newbold/EyeEm/Getty Images; p. 127: JGI/Tom Grill/Blend Images/Getty Images; p. 130: Joos Mind/Taxi/Getty Images.